The Gospel Takes Roots on Kilimanjaro

Kachere Series
P.O. Box 1037, Zomba, Malawi
kachere@globemw.net
www.sdnp.org.mw/kachereseries/

Copyright 2006 Klaus Fiedler

All rights reserved. No part of this publication may be reproduced, stored in a retrieval system, or transmitted in any form or by any means, electronic, mechanical, photocopying, recording or otherwise, without prior permission from the publishers.

Published by
Kachere Series
P.O. Box 1037, Zomba, Malawi

ISBN 99908-76-08-8
Kachere Monograph 23
ISBN-13: 978-99908-76-08-6

The Kachere Series is represented outside Africa by:
African Books Collective Oxford (orders@africanbookscollective.com)
Michigan State University Press East Lansing (msupress@msu.edu)

Layout and Cover design: Mercy Chilunga
Cover picture: Leipzig Mission (Church bell and house of a Christian family, around 1920)

Printed by Lightning Source

The Gospel Takes Roots on Kilimanjaro

A History of the Evangelical – Lutheran Church of
Old Moshi-Mbokomu (1885 - 1940)

Klaus Fiedler

Kachere Monographs no. 23

Kachere Series
Zomba
2006

Kachere Series
P.O. Box 1037, Zomba, Malawi
kachere@globemw.net
www.sdnp.org.mw/kachereseries/

This book is part of the Kachere Series, a range of books on religion, culture, and society from Malawi. Other titles are:

Klaus Fiedler, *The Story of Faith Missions: From Hudson Taylor to Present Day Africa*

Klaus Fiedler, *Teaching Church History in Malawi*

John McCracken, *Politics & Christianity in Malawi 1875-1940: The Impact of the Livingstonia Mission in the Northern Province*

Andrew C. Ross, *Blantyre Mission and the Making of Modern Malawi*

George Shepperson and Thomas Price, *Independent African: John Chilembwe and the Nyasaland Rising of 1915*

Rachel Nyagondwe Banda, *Women of Bible and Culture: Baptist Convention Women in Southern Malawi*

Rachel Nyagondwe Fiedler, *Coming of Age: A Christianized Initiation among Women in Southern Malawi*

James Tengatenga, *Church, State and Society in Malawi: The Anglican Case*

Helen E.P. van Koevering, *Dancing their Dreams: The Lakeshore Nyanja Women of the Anglican Diocese of Niassa*

Yonah Hisbon Matemba, *Matandani: The Second Adventist Mission in Malawi*

Margaret Sinclair, *Salt and Light: The Letters of Jack and Mamie Martin in Malawi 1921-28*

Steven Paas, *The Faith Moves South. A History of the Church in Africa*

The Kachere Series is the publications arm of the Department of Theology and Religious Studies of the University of Malawi

Series Editors: J.C. Chakanza, F.L. Chingota, Klaus Fiedler, P.A. Kalilombe, Chimwemwe Katumbi, Martin Ott, Shareef Mohammad

Foreword

This is a book that addresses three continents. That is not wrong, since they were all involved. The centre of it all is of course in Africa, on the densely populated slopes of Mt Kilimanjaro, where bananas and coffee flourish. There you find what was, when the 19th century turned into the 20th, Moshi chiefdom, and a little to the west, Mbokomu chiefdom, two of the several chiefdoms of the Chagga, living above the plains and below the forest belt and the bare upper reaches of the mountain.

Here at Moshi (since the town was established in the plains, people say "Old Moshi") the Chagga welcomed the first Christian missionaries to live with them in 1885, the beginning of their turning to the Christian faith. Three generations later I had the privilege, while living and working at the other end in the south of Tanzania, to visit, stay for some time and write the history of Old Moshi congregation up to 1940. I am grateful for the information and insights the people of the Old Moshi Lutheran congregations shared with me, and for their hospitality.

Europe is also involved in this story. Of course, all the early missionaries were *azungu*, and in this case they came from Germany. Their work was appreciated, but one of them was more famous than the others: Bruno Gutmann. He was so well accepted among the Chagga, that, 40 years later, I was told that "he spoke better Chagga then we ourselves did". Gutmann entered deeply into Chagga culture, and, on the base of this identification, he became perhaps the most famous German missiologist of his times.

Asia is involved, too. Not only that Jesus was born in Asia and lived all his life on earth there, but the Leipzig Mission began its work in North Tanzania after two generations of missionary work among the Tamil in Southern India, starting in 1840. And it was there that Karl Graul, the early Director of Leipzig Mission, developed his theology of incorporating as much as possible of a local culture into the life of the Christian church. Three Tamil Christians came over from India to assist in the building of the first structures for the Lutheran missionaries (including one house in Old Moshi), and Bruno Gutmann himself had originally wanted to go to India to work as a missionary there.

Though Asia and Europe are involved, this is essentially an African story, because crucial is not the Gospel that the missionaries brought, but the Gospel that the Chagga received. And receive it, they did.

The Early Years

1. The First Contacts of the Chagga with Christianity

The first contact was made possible when chief Masaki of Kilema received Johannes Rebmann[1] in 1849 and sent him on to Machame. Rebmann passed above Moshi. His stay was too short to make the Chagga understand the Gospel.[2] Since that year the Chagga were on the missionary map.[3] In 1878 CMS missionaries from Freetown sent greetings to Rindi with an Arab trader. Rindi sent a letter in reply asking the CMS to establish a mission, and Lamb, missionary of Freretown, sent a Bible to him.[4]

In 1885 (17.-26.3.) Bishop Hannington of the Church Missionary Society (CMS) came to Moshi to introduce Fitch and Wray to chief Rindi, who gave to the mission a plot on Kitimbirihu. In 1888 Taylor came, but the first missionary really to stay at Moshi and to learn the Chagga language was Steggall, who stayed from 1889 to 1892,[5] started a school, built a church and held regular Sunday services, and when Bishop Tucker visited Moshi in 1892, the first two Chagga were baptized (21.2.1882).[6]

Meanwhile Rindi had died and his son and successor Meli was not willing to accept German rule in the same way as his father had done, so the Germans tried to subdue him by force and attacked Moshi on the 10.6.1892 and were completely defeated. Steggall had tried in vain to mediate, and his sheer presence must have been an affront to the German government because the Chagga trusted Steggall, and during the conflict, when no white man could venture out of camp unless accompanied by a substantial number of

---

[1] Rebmann was a (German) missionary of the (British) Church Missionary Society (CMS), working at the Kenya coast. He was the first European to see Mt Kilimanjaro. When he reported that he had seen snow on it, the famous German geographers did not believe him, since they knew for sure that under the Equator there can be no snow in Africa.

[2] Bruno Gutmann, *Unter dem Trutzbaum – Eine Einkehr in Moshi am Kilimanjaro*, Leipzig: Verlag der Ev.-Luth. Mission, nd. [1938], p. 71.

[3] Cf. Bengt Sundkler and Christopher Steed, *A History of the Church in Africa*, Cambridge University Press,[2] 2001, p. 547.

[4] Freretown, situated opposite Mombasa Island on the shore, was founded in 1874 as a settlement for freed slaves (Bengt Sundkler and Christopher Steed, *A History of the Church in Africa*, Cambridge University Press,[2] 2001, p. 553; Gustav Warneck, *Abriß einer Geschichte der protestantischen Missionen von der Reformation bis auf die Gegenwart*, Berlin: Martin Warneck, 1910, p. 321).

[5] Bruno Gutmann, *Unter dem Trutzbaum*, p. 17.

[6] Paul Fleisch, *Hundert Jahre lutherischer Mission*, Leipzig: Verlag der Ev.-Luth. Mission, 1936, p. 267.

soldiers, he travelled to and fro without ever being armed. So the government demanded his withdrawal and the CMS complied under protest.[7]
When Steggall was forced to withdraw, there were two Chagga Christians, Samweli Tanga and Thomas and several pupils. Samuel Tanga accompanied Steggall to Taveta, returned to Moshi in 1905, where he died in 1925 as a faithful Christian. Thomas returned to his traditional religion, later became an assistant to Chief Kawina, attended services occasionally, but never found his way back to Christianity. He was hanged with his chief in 1901.[8]
In December 1892 the Anglican Church Missionary Society handed over Moshi mission to the Lutheran Leipzig Mission,[9] and their first missionaries under the leadership of Traugott Päsler arrived at Mombasa on 12.7.1893. When they got word that the Germans on 12.8.1893 had reconquered Moshi, they started out, reaching the plot where Steggall had lived on Kitimbirihu on 30.9.1893. Finding all buildings destroyed and conditions in general still quite unsettled, they decided to establish their first station not at Moshi but at Machame (5.10.1893). The next mission was Mamba (26.6.1894). At Moshi the mission was reestablished on the 11.2.1896 by Faßmann and Segebrock, not at Kitimbirihu, but on Mungu, a formerly sacred forest of the Moshi chiefdom where the initiation ceremonies had been taking place.[10] The response of the local population was quicker than at Mamba and Machame, after only a month a school was started, not on the request of the missionaries but on request of some of the former pupils of Steggall. And the first baptism in the Leipzig mission did not take place on one of their older missions but at Old Moshi, when four pupils of the boarding school were baptized, two of whom had learned to read with Steggall. Most prominent among them was Msando Kimambo (Yohane), and Steggall came over from Taveta to attend their baptism.[11]

2. What did the Mission mean for the Chagga?

Chief Rindi had not called the CMS because of a deep religious interest, but because he wanted to enhance his position among the Chagga chiefs.

---

[7] Roland Oliver, *The Missionary Factor in East Africa*, London, ²1965 (1952), p. 166.
[8] Bruno Gutmann, *Unter dem Trutzbaum*, p. 35, Minutes elders 3.6.1911.
[9] Bruno Gutmann, *Unter dem Trutzbaum*, p. 20. At that occasion the Leipzig Mission emphasized that they were not taking over the mission to serve the German Empire nor the colonial movement, but to serve the Kingdom of God (Paul Fleisch, *Hundert Jahre lutherischer Mission*, p. 267).
[10] Bruno Gutmann, *Unter dem Trutzbaum*, p. 8-15.
[11] Paul Fleisch, *Hundert Jahre lutherischer Mission*, p. 270.

Whereas the chief welcomed the mission as a political force he could use, it was not so welcome to those powerful in Chagga society because the mission provided ways of social mobility, which were outside their control. However, it was for this reason that the underprivileged in society were attracted, like Yohane Kimambo, one of the future leaders of the congregation: his parents had both died when he was around six years old, and he was cared for by a relative of his. When he was ten, he was often sent to work as a "boy" for the German soldiers in order to earn something. There he saw for the first time that children of his age group were wearing clothes whereas he was going naked still, because his relatives gave him only his food. He thought: "If I go on to live with them, I shall always remain poor just as my father was". So he decided to work as a "boy" for the German soldiers in order to earn something. Very soon after the Leipzig Mission came to Moshi he started to work for them and to learn to read (2.3.1896). Msando Kimambo was the first to ask for baptism and was baptized together with three others on 20.1.1898 and took the name Yohane.[12] It is clear that the chance to improve his social status had attracted him to work for and read with the mission. But there he found something else: Contrary to the soldiers, he heard the missionaries pray and he thought: "They pray nearly as we do".[13] His case is only one of many similar cases.

The first to join the mission were those who had no status in society, mostly orphans. They had little to loose, and in the mission they saw a chance to move upwards on the social ladder. They were able to acquire some clothes, to save up for their bride wealth, maybe even to buy cattle. Thus a new element of mobility was introduced into Chagga society, and a new élite began to emerge, e.g. those who had acquired certain new skills at the mission and who worked for it, mainly as teachers. In this way people from unimportant families or clans became leaders, for example Imanuel Mkony and those from the Njau clan.

But not only non-religious motives made the Chagga open to accept Christianity. Yohane Kimambo's testimony shows that he realized a relatedness between Christianity and Chagga religion. So did others. In addition to this, Chagga religion and its social sanctions were no longer unquestioningly accepted. This is shown by the many customs which Chief Rindi changed (and by changing these customs he also changed their religious side), for example when he threw the pots in which the war medicine was kept down

---

[12] Paul Fleisch, *Hundert Jahre lutherischer Mission*, p. 270 gives 30.1.1898.
[13] Bruno Gutmann, "Johane Kimambo, ein Jünger ohne Falsch", *Afrikanische Charakterköpfe: Unseres Heilands schwarze Handlanger*, Leipzig 1922, p. 45.

into the ravine, thus making the sacred forest useless, later to be used for the building of the first church on Kitimbirihu. Thus the political, the social and the religious situation all provided a good ground for acceptance of the Christian faith.

For the first years the main activity of the missionaries concentrated on the schools. Compared with other missions the erecting of the buildings provided little contact with the local population as most of the work was done by a group of Tamil Christians from South India (three masons, all brothers: Sinnappen, Rajappen and Joseph with their catechist Zechariahs[14]) assisted by Swahili from the coast. But school was taken up wholeheartedly (not only being offered by the mission but also eagerly accepted by a growing number of Chagga) and provided much of the initial contact with the population.

First came the boarding school. The first pupils were children who worked for the mission and were also taught to read every day a few hours. They lived at the mission, were fed and clothed there and received a small, but for them considerable, remuneration in cash. This gave them social status in Chagga society and made Christianity much more acceptable also for those having a certain social status.

Right from the start it was the missionaries' intention to start a school at the chief's court. The chief was not interested, but due to pressure from the German officials he asked for a school to be established at his court at Mahoma in 1897.[15] Meli did not come often, and he showed no interest at all in the boarding school, but still the school could not accept all those who were interested in entering.

These two small schools had far reaching results. The school at the chief's never really got off the ground under Meli,[16] but it was important in that it provided an official sanction for the new custom of going to school. The boarding school was a success in itself. Pupils really learnt to read, and from the boarding school came the first converts. Four pupils were baptized on 20.1.1998.[17] More were under instruction. From these pupils and converts came the first teacher evangelists, who were to become so important for the evangelization of the Chagga. Besides this the school provided an example of success. People could see that it was a useful thing to go to school. For example Petro Masamu entered school as an orphan on the lowest reaches of

---

[14] Bruno Gutmann, *Unter dem Trutzbaum*, pp. 5-8.
[15] Diary Moshi Dec. 1897 - Dec 1902, in Johanna Eggert, *Missionsschule und sozialer Wandel in Ostafrika*, Bielefeld: Bertelsmann, 1970, p. 184.
[16] Even worse was the fate of the school at the government station. (Paul Fleisch, *Hundert Jahre lutherischer Mission*, p. 276).
[17] Paul Fleisch, *Hundert Jahre lutherischer Mission*, p. 270 gives 30.1.1898.

the social ladder, but within a few years he had become a teacher, a man with a leading place in society.[18]

3. Expansion beyond the mission station

As soon as the first pupils had completed their course, schools were established outside the mission. But there it was no longer the missionary who taught but former boarding school pupils. The first schools were established at Tela, Shia and Mbokomu,[19] all places that were roughly at the same altitude range as Kidia. They were established on the request of the local population (Tela and Shia) or on the request of the chief of Mbokomu, the neighbouring chiefdom.

With the establishment of the school at Mbokomu the church had entered a new chiefdom, and how this school came to be established is an interesting example of social mobility made possible through the work of the mission. Msami, a man from Moshi of low social status, but who had learned to read, refused to work for the chief, so he was deprived of his plot and emigrated to Mbokomu, where, as a reader, he gained high status at the chief's court. He influenced the chief to build a school in 1901,[20] in which soon Yohane Kimambo and Petro (Tarawia) Masane, former boarding school pupils, taught 30-40 children.[21]

4. Deeper Outreach into Society

Around 1900 the mission began to become a force within society, no longer at the fringe of it. This can be seen in the fact that at this time even parents with a good social status began to send their children to the boarding school. Also Christianity began to become interesting to people not living at the mission. In 1900 there were three such candidates for baptism,[22] and in 1901 the first complete family not living at the mission was baptized. Also interest arose among women. In 1900 a boarding school for girls was opened with four pupils.

It was in these ways that a Christian community came into existence. This community was somewhat independent, as it had its centre outside of the social structure of the Chagga, but as most of its converts did not leave

---

[18] Interview Ndesanjo Kitange 27.5.1971.
[19] Paul Fleisch, *Hundert Jahre lutherischer Mission*, p. 276.
[20] Diary Moshi Feb 1901 in Johanna Eggert, *Missionsschule und sozialer Wandel in Ostafrika*, p. 184.
[21] Paul Fleisch, *Hundert Jahre lutherischer Mission*, p. 276.
[22] Paul Fleisch, *Hundert Jahre lutherischer Mission*, p. 277.

their surroundings, this new community remained closely integrated into the whole of Chagga society. In 1904 the congregation consisted of 148 people,[23] and it was quite an impressive community. It held the monopoly of education, the key to progress. They had paid employment, another key to progress. Not only that, among the Christians there was better health, for example child mortality fell sharply from 70-80% over the years, and even their monogamous marriages proved quite fertile. Thus the Christian community was very modern and very attractive to socially mobile people, a thing that has changed since then.

But the attraction of the Christian community also clearly was of a religious nature as they followed a religion that answered so many of men's questions far better than tribal religion did.

5. The Growth of the Congregation 1906-1914

At Easter 1906 thirty-four adults were baptized, but the year of 1907 showed a decline, the process of Christianization loosing momentum a little, and traditional religion gaining new strength. In 1908 only 25 adults were baptized, and only 8 in 1909. There were also changes in personnel, in 1908 Faßmann, the founder, left and Johannes Schanz took over, leaving in 1910 to be replaced by Bruno Gutmann.

This slowdown was followed by a real upsurge in numbers of those who wanted to join the church. In 1912 there were 12 candidates too old to walk to the mission, so that they had to be taught in their homes. On Christmas 1913 183 people were baptized. The congregation had 849 members, something like 10% of the population of Moshi.[24] As there was an average of 1200 people attending the Sunday services and 934 children were enrolled in twelve schools, at least a quarter of the population was under direct Christian influence.[25]

6. The Work of the Teachers

The success of the missionary work was mainly due to the teachers. They were all local in the sense that Faßmann himself taught the first pupils at the boarding school, and asked the best to help him teach. At first they received no formal training. Immanuel Mkony relates: "I was taught at school and I

---

[23] Paul Fleisch, *Hundert Jahre lutherischer Mission*, p. 277.
[24] Paul Fleisch, *Hundert Jahre lutherischer Mission*, p. 287.
[25] Paul Fleisch, *Hundert Jahre lutherischer Mission*, p. 287.

also taught my fellow pupils a little."[26] Very soon this proved insufficient, and the Leipzig Mission opened a teacher training course at Moshi under Johannes Raum with ten students,[27] among them four from Moshi and Mbokomu: Yohane Kimambo (Mbokomu); Petro Masamu (Tela), Anton Tarimo (Mahoma) and Zakaria Ringo (Tsunduny). They all completed the course successfully in 1905. Yohane Kimambo was posted to Kidia, Petro Masamu to Tela, Anton Tarimo to Shia and Zakaria Ringo as well to Kidia.[28] From 1904-1907 the second course (and the last one at Moshi) was held. Three students from Moshi took part: Simeon Macha (Tsunduny), Davidi Mtee (Tela) and one more, most probably Paulo Msaki.[29] The first four teachers all came from the boarding school and were orphans in addition to that. One of then, Anton Moshi came from the royal clan.[30] Of the second group Davidi Mtee was an orphan, but not Zakaria Ringo of the first group, whose father was a local doctor.[31] In order to understand a little better the work done by those first seminary trained teachers, here are in short some biographies.

Yohane Kimambo: born around 1885, from Mbokomu, both parents died when he was around six years old, boarding school 1896, baptized 20.1.1898, assistant teacher, seminary Moshi 1902 - 1905, for more than 10 years head teacher of Kidia school. In Gutmann's opinion he was the most effective teacher among his contemporaries. During the First World War he retired from schoolwork, as he was not strong enough to teach (without salary) and to cultivate his fields so as to feed his family. When the German missionaries had to leave, he took, together with Filipo Njau, Gutmann's place. After Gutmann's return he was teacher at Mbokomu.

Petro Masamu: boarding school, assistant teacher, opened work at Tela, taught 1901 in Mbokomu, seminary 1902-1905, posted to Tela where he lived and worked until his retirement.

Zakaria Ringo: Seminary Moshi 1902-1905, posted to Shia. Left work after the First World War to go to Kenya. Returned when Zeilinger came.

---

[26] Interview Immanuel Mkony 26.7.1971.
[27] Paul Fleisch, *Hundert Jahre lutherischer Mission*, p. 277. One of the ten students (Danieli from Mwika) did not finish the course and left his Christian faith.
[28] Paul Fleisch, *Hundert Jahre lutherischer Mission*, p. 298 .wrongly states that Yohane Kimambo was placed to Mbokomu. See Bruno Gutmann, "Johane Kimambo, ein Jünger ohne Falsch", *Afrikanische Charakterköpfe: Unseres Heilands schwarze Handlanger*, Leipzig 1922, pp. 43-45.
[29] Interview Ndesanjo Kitange 27.5.1972.
[30] He was either called Anton Tarimo or Anton Moshi.
[31] Interview Ndesanjo Kitange 27.5.1972.

The first teacher to live at Kahe. Afterwards evangelist (who did not teach school) at Shia. Retirement, died 1969= =.

Davidi Mtee: Seminary 1904-1907, taught at Mowo. Died in 1919 of malaria.

Imanuel Mkony: Orphan from Mbokomu. 1900 boarding school, taught at Tela, Mowo, Mahoma. Lived on the mission, married an orphan (who had been cared for by missionaries). Although he was interested in going to the seminary he was not sent. When Gutmann came, he asked to be sent, but Gutmann refused, saying: "be content with what you have"[32]. Took growing part in the work of the church at Kidia. In 1923 he started the work at Kahe together with Anton Tarimo, from where he got malaria that never really left him. When Filipo Njau left for Marangu Seminary, Imanuel Mkony became Gutmann's assistant. Elected almost unopposed for the first ordination course. Acquired a plot at Tela on Gutmann's advice, where he retired.

These teachers, seminary trained and not seminary trained, did not only do all the schoolwork and most of the work of the church, they were also a leading élite, especially those trained at the seminary. They were most open to modern values, they had a wider horizon, spoke and wrote Swahili, knew English and some of them even German, they built Swahili houses etc. They were the most modern group in society, quite influential, and from them later was to come the strongest reaction to Gutmann's conservative attitudes.

The teachers normally preached on Sundays at their outstations and provided most of the pastoral care for the Christians at their respective places. Some of them were judged to be able in both preaching and pastoral care. But the idea of preparing them for ordination that Gutmann had in 1910 (though not to train them at once for ordination, first make the best of them catechists) was rejected and no steps were taken into this direction until the 1930s.

7. Literature

There was another setback. All the years the Old Moshi congregation had hardly any literature. Faßmann had translated the Gospel of John, Raum had produced a book of biblical stories and in 1910 Schanz' translation of Mark was published. Hymnbook and New Testament were published only in the

---

[32] Interview Immanuel Mkoyi, 25.5.1971.

1930s.[33] In addition to this there were simple schoolbooks and a monthly paper (*Mbuya ya Vandu Vuu*, Friend of the Black People). This was very little, but this scarcity had the advantage of forcing the people to be more open to the use of Swahili.

8. Major Events Around 1910

For the congregation the years after 1904 were years of quiet development, the church was growing; there were few changes in personnel and no serious troubles from outside. But a few events should be mentioned.

In 1907 the boarding school for boys was closed, as it was no longer needed. Around 1908 the first Christian children began to become of age and the congregation had to make provision for them to be instructed in the Christian faith and to be prepared to receive Holy Communion for the first time. But what troubled Christians more was the issue if their children should be circumcised.[34]

The first decade in the 20th century was a time of growing influence from the wider world, represented by the development of (New) Moshi (rail head and seat of government), the growth of the money economy and the (still limited) impact of Islam.

It is into such a situation that Bruno Gutmann came to Old Moshi, in 1910, already an experienced missionary, in full command of the Chagga language and with deep interest in and appreciation for Chagga culture. He had come to Tanzania in 1902, had worked first at Mamba, then (1904) in Machame. In 1906 he was given the task of founding a new mission, Masama in South Machame. In 1908 he had gone to Germany for health reasons, and ten months after his return he was posted to Old Moshi.

For his work as a missionary he had received a solid training at the Lutheran Leipzig Mission Seminary, supplemented by some courses at the University. He had accepted the Lutheran theological concept of the *adiaphora*, the things in between", which allow a missionary and the church to distin-

---

[33] Bruno Gutmann (ed), *Kitabu kya siri [Book of the Congregation]*, Moshi/Mbokomu 1931, *Mkundana Mhya fu mbike ni Mndumi odu Yesu Kristo*, Stuttgart: Bibelanstalt 1939.

[34] The Chagga had originally a large number of transition rites, not only for the major transitions like birth, puberty, marriage and death, but also for many events in between, for example the *mrighorigho*-rite to mark the end of childhood at the age of about 10, the removal of the lower incisors at the age of about 12 and a few years later the piercing of the ear and many others. Some of these transition rituals had quietly declined, but especially circumcision was strongly adhered to, both for girls and boys. (All these rites for boys, with the appropriate teachings both in Chagga and German, are recorded in Bruno Gutmann, *Die Stammeslehren der Dschagga*, 3 vols., München: C.H. Beck'sche Verlangsbuchhandlung, 1932, 1935, 1938, 2028 pp).

guish between things that are intrinsically bad, intrinsically good, and those in between. Much of culture could be classified as *adiaphora*, as neither intrinsically good nor bad. Such cultural elements would therefore be entrusted to the church's scrutiny and care: care to preserve all that is good, and scrutiny to reform any element that is not or no longer useful and appropriate to the Christian faith.

Gutmann's approach in his missionary work can be rightly called the "cultural approach", because he saw Chagga culture (and any other culture) as a divine gift, not untainted by sin, but still able to provide the ground into which the seed of the Gospel could be planted.

Coming to Terms with Chagga Culture

Right after his arrival Gutmann had to apply his concept of not unduly disturbing traditional culture to the thorny issue of female circumcision.

1. Female circumcision[1]

The African leaders of the church had touched the issue at a meeting at Moshi some time before, but had shelved it because there were not yet any children of that age. Unfortunately they had forgotten Ndeterewio Kafui,[2] the daughter of Gabrieli Maro, from Sangu, the easternmost branch of the Moshi congregation. Gabriele Maro had moved there from Mahoma where he had become a Christian.[3] He was in doubt if it would be proper for him as a Christian to have his daughter circumcised, so he brought the matter up for discussion in the elders' meeting of 3.5.1910.[4] It is not stated who had put the doubt in his mind, but most probably not Schanz, because for him the question came completely unexpected. Schanz, then missionary in charge, looked first for direction from Leipzig, but could not find any.[5] The matter was obviously discussed at some length. Two observations on the elders' attitude are interesting, first that the elders could not be made to see a difference between boys' and girls' circumcision. Second that they showed some willingness to abolish circumcision for Christian children, both male and female. To the last point Schanz made a note to the effect that the elders did not seem to have realized the difficulties of abolishing circumcision.[6] As Schanz knew of no authoritative decision from Leipzig, he asked Superintendent Müller who replied that in 1906 the matter had come up for discus-

---

[1] The most famous controversy about female circumcision took place in Kenya, where several missions led by the Presbyterians and the Africa Inland Mission forbade female circumcision. For a full treatment see: Jocelyn Murray, The Kikuyu Female Circumcision Controversy: with Special Reference to the Church Missionary Society's Sphere of Influence, PhD, UCLA, 1974. For a brief treatment and context see: Klaus Fiedler, *The Story of Faith Missions. From Hudson Taylor to Present Day Africa*, Oxford et al: 1994, pp. 252-256.
[2] Name kindly supplied by J.C. Winter, 24.1.1974.
[3] With him went a few other Christians, for example Yohane and Isaki Tilya from Kidia. This meant the beginning of the church there. Interview Ndesanjo Kitange 27.5.1972.
[4] Minutes elders 3.5.1910.
[5] Minutes elders 26.7.1910.
[6] Minutes elders 3.5.1910.

sion but that Leipzig had refused to agree to a prohibition of circumcision.[7] Therefore Schanz, directed by Müller, looked for another authority. During the church elders' meeting at Moshi referred to above the matter had been discussed and Müller had heard that the elders on their own account had banned circumcision. But the Moshi elders who had been present at that meeting knew nothing of such a ban, and since they had forgotten Nderewio Kafui, Schanz asked Gabrieli Maro to make her wait until a final decision had been reached. He promised to ask Gutmann to make sure that a decision might be taken soon.[8] For Gabrieli Kimari it must have been hard to wait such a long time, and no doubt even more for his daughter, and on 16.12.1910 he asked again and Gutmann told him that there would be no objection to his daughter being circumcised "as long as everything pagan would be avoided".[9]

2. Confirmation, another Transition Rite

Less than a year later steps had to be taken to start the first confirmation class. Gutmann opened this first course with a special service in the presence of parents and sponsors,[10] and this foreshadowed the great emphasis that Gutmann was later going to lay on confirmation. The children were taught two periods a week, one of them after the Sunday service.

With confirmation a second transition rite parallel to that of circumcision was introduced, but nothing was done to bring them together in any way. In this area of major significance the Christians were left to decide for themselves what was compatible with Christianity, though they were guided firmly in many minor matters. This shows clearly that the missionaries were in a dilemma not knowing what to do, so they escaped into this broad rule of "avoiding everything pagan". But this also had its advantages in that it left much room for the individual's strength and in that it avoided unnecessary clashes, but later it also made possible the circumcision controversy of the 1920s.

---

[7] During the controversy on female circumcision among the Kikuyu the attitude of the missionaries was exactly the opposite. For a discussion of this and related issues, see: Klaus Fiedler, "Bishop Lucas' Christianization of Traditional Rites, the Kikuyu Female Circumcision Controversy and the 'Cultural Approach' of Conservative German Missionaries in Tanzania", in Noel Q. King and Klaus Fiedler (eds.), *Robin Lamburn – From a Missionary's Notebook: the Yao of Tunduru and Other Essays*, Saarbrücken/Ft. Lauderdale, 1991, pp. 207-217.
[8] Minutes elders 26.7.1910.
[9] Minutes elders 16.12.1910.
[10] Minutes elders 3.6.1911.

3. The Growing Influence of European Civilization

At the turn of the 19th to the 20th century Chagga contact to European civilization had had already a long history, but around 1900 this contact made itself felt with new vigour. Since 1901 the Kilimanjaro region had been pacified. An increasing number of European settlers moved into the plains below the area where the Chagga lived on the slopes of Mt Kilimanjaro,[11] thus providing alternative employment to that provided by the mission and the colonial government. In 1908 a telegraph connection was established, in 1911 the railway from Tanga reached New Moshi. This contact to European civilization was another agent of change in Chagga society. Up to then the missionaries, who had brought European culture, had filtered it, had tried to pass on to the Chagga only what they felt was compatible with Christianity. Now this European civilization became increasingly a force of its own. The relationship became triangular, Chagga society and religion were faced with a double challenge from the mission and from "town", but also the church was faced with a double challenge from traditional society and from Western secular society, and the question was: with what side would the church align itself, with traditional society or with Western progress. During the first decade of missionary work there had been a clear alliance with Western progress, mainly through the fact that jobs provided by the mission absorbed many of the early converts, thus opening them for all kinds of new ideas. What reinforced this alliance was the fact that during the first decade the Christian leaders were the teacher-evangelists.

But the church was out to win the whole of Chagga society, not to win and advance just a small group. So the influx of converts who had not lived at the mission necessarily brought about a rapprochement with Chagga traditional society. Another factor leading into the same direction was the organization of the congregation in 1904. The congregation got a council of elders as the policy making body, whose authority was above that of the teachers. During the years before World War I these elders were comparatively young, but nevertheless more conservative than the teachers had been. And as there were no voluntary organizations within the church, it was hard to integrate the progressive element, created by the mission and doing most of the church's work, into the church, and it was here that the rift between pro-

---

[11] One episode of this is reported in Bruno Gutmann, "Wie ich den Buren begegnete", *Evg.-Luth. Missionsblatt*, 1905, pp. 446-452. At that time Gutmann had the hope that these settlers would be of some profit for the Chagga on the slopes of Mt Kilimanjaro. The missionary editor added a precautionary note, and this was obviously what Gutmann thought later himself.

gress and church leadership started at Moshi. This rift was small at the beginning, but was widened deliberately by Gutmann when he took over. Between the wars it became quite large.

Bruno Gutmann's Impact 1910–1914

When Gutmann took over Old Moshi he had already been a missionary among the Chagga for eight years, and what was more important, he had a clear analysis of the situation and a clear concept for his work, a concept clearly distinguishable from that of his two predecessors.[1] But his ideas were also unexpected for the congregation as a whole and contrary to the deepest aspiration of some of its most progressive members.

1. Gutmann's Analysis of the Situation and his Aims

In his analysis Gutmann clearly stated the enemies of the work of the church: Firstly Islam. There was a majority of Muslims at the government station, all chiefs' representatives there had become Muslims and there were already some Muslim families among the Chagga even in their home areas on the mountain. Gutmann saw Islam on the offensive, even against Christians. But as a much more formidable enemy he saw European civilization, because it destroyed the tribal organism destined by God to be the vessel to receive the Gospel.[2] He was aware that European civilization was mainly being brought by government and European settlers by providing paid employment, but he claimed that even the mission brought the evils of civilization, for example by training local carpenters and thereby making them depend on money and uprooting them from the firm ground of Chagga tribal society.[3] This analysis of the situation Gutmann never changed, though the threat of Islam became less after the First World War, and he ceased to make much mention of it after that.[4]

Gutmann saw as the aim of his missionary work the folk church (*Volkskirche*). A folk church was to be a church not composed of individual con-

---

[1] His analysis of the situation and his concepts can be deducted from an article he published, which is written in a programmatic way: Bruno Gutmann, "Die gegenwärtige Lage der Dschaggamission", *Jahrbuch der sächsischen Missionskonferenz*, 1912. The article was actually written in 1911, and since it looks like being the result of much thinking, it can be taken well as reflecting Gutmann's ideas in 1910.

[2] Bruno Gutmann, "Die gegenwärtige Lage der Dschaggamission", p. 63. Gutmann never wavered in his opposition to and denunciation of European civilization, which he saw as a destructive force. In his only article written in English, he calls European civilization "a blatant blasphemy" ("The African Standpoint", *Journal of the International Institute of African Languages and Cultures*, vol. 8, January 1935, no. 1, pp. 1-17).

[3] Bruno Gutmann, "Die Gegenwärtige Lage der Dschaggamission", p. 65.

[4] In almost all of Africa the spread of Islam stopped between 1900 and 1920.

verts but of converted Christians, who retained most of their former social ties.

Since Gustav Warneck, German Protestant missionaries almost unanimously agreed that the aim of all missionary work was to establish a "folk church".[5] Most of them had no clear definition of the term, but Gutmann did have a clear definition, and as so often, he used the same term his fellow missionaries used, but filled it with a considerably different meaning: For him a folk church is a church clearly and positively related to the folkhood (*Volkstum*) of a nation or of an ethnic group. This folkhood he defined not as folklore, but as the primal ties (*urtümliche Bindungen*)[6] of kinship, neighbourhood and age group, which he understood as being divine institutions. Thus a folk church is a church that cares for everything that is good in the social order, but especially it cares for the clan that it will survive and for the neighbourhood that it will be a reality.[7] It is a church that uses the primal ties to fulfill the mission of the church and that instructs its converts to serve these primal ties and to help to preserve them.[8] For Gutmann this folk church was to be a Lutheran church, again in the sense he understood the word "Lutheran". For Gutmann the Lutheran interpretation of the Gospel was unquestioningly the deepest and the final one. Being Lutheran meant for him the full acceptance of the Augsburg Confession as the doctrinal basis and of Luther's Small Catechism for the instruction of Christians.[9] This also meant for him to stress the importance of the congregation, and to underplay the importance of the individual in contrast with Pietism and revival piety. It also meant a careful attitude towards the *adiaphora*, that means things and

---

[5] Gustav Warneck (1834-1910) was the leading German Protestant missiologist during the great days of the Christian mission at the turn from the 19th to the 20th century. His most famous book is *Evangelische Missionslehre*, [Protestant Missiology], 5 vols., Gotha, 1897-1903. He also wrote the standard German mission history: *Abriß einer Geschichte der protestantischen Mission*, Berlin 1882.

[6] Elsewhere the translation of *urtümliche Bindungen* is primordial ties. This seems to me to imply an emphasis on things of long ago, whereas 'primal ties' emphasizes that they are still the base of all human life.

[7] Of the three primal ties, Gutmann paid least attention to the primal tie of the age-group.

[8] Gutmann never wrote a systematic missiology, but published a number of books which deal with his missionary work in Moshi and in the course of that discuss wider missiological issues. Most important are: *Das Dschaggaland und seine Christen*, Leipzig, 1925; *Gemeindeaufbau aus dem Evangelium*, Leipzig, 1925; *Freies Menschentum aus ewigen Bindungen*, Kassel, 1928.

[9] Luther's Minor Catechism and the Augsburg Confession were included into the hymnbook of Old Moshi congregation: Bruno Gutmann (ed.), *Kitabu kya siri [Book of the Congregation]*, Moshi/Mbokomu 1931.

institutions that were neither intrinsically good nor bad like beer, transition rites, dances, etc.[10]

When discussing the enemies of missionary work it is telling that he does not mention Chagga religion. Nor does he speak of dark heathenism or something like that. That reflects to some extent that the outcome of the contest between Traditional Religion and Christianity had already been decided, but far more that he saw the relationship between Christianity and African Traditional Religion rather in terms of fulfillment than of conquest.[11] His aim therefore is to connect the new to the old and to avoid disrupting society by changing its religion. He demanded that the Gospel had to be welded firmly to the folkhood of the Chagga.[12] By this he barred a development of the church into a somewhat democratic direction and bound the church more to the old order.

One way of dealing with challenges of those years, western secularism, the growing numbers and the rise of the young generation, was to weld the church firmly into Chagga culture, its "folkhood". The other way of dealing with these challenges was to organize the congregation, not just as far as prescribed by the constitution of the Chagga churches as agreed to by the missionaries' conference in 1903,[13] which provided only for the offices of the elders, the pastor and the treasurer (the last two posts then always being held by the missionary in charge).[14] Many more new (unpaid) offices would have to be introduced, the office bearers working not on behalf of the missionary but on behalf of the congregation. For these offices again the existing structures of Chagga folkhood had to be utilized as far as possible.[15]

This church was to be so rooted in Chagga culture that it should develop as an organic extension of that culture. To achieve this an educational process would be necessary. Gutmann did not want this to be based primarily on western type of schooling but on the Chagga traditional pattern of education

---

[10] A discussion of this concept is: Bruno Gutmann, "Von Ihnen nach Außen – der lutherischer Weg", *Evangelisch-Lutherische Kirchenzeitung*, 1954, pp. 305-309.

[11] The idea that Christianity is the fulfillment of African Traditional Religion, finds expression in articles like: "Der Zug des Vaters zum Sohne im Volkstum der Wadschagga" (Gutmann, *Das Dschaggaland und seine Christen*, pp. 132-139) and "Die religiös-sittlichen Eigenwerte der noch natürlich gebundenen Völker als Aufbaustoffe im Wurzelboden für das Evangelium" (Gutmann, *Gemeindeaufbau aus dem Evangelium*, pp. 64-68).

[12] Bruno Gutmann, "Die gegenwärtige Lage der Dschaggamission".

[13] Minutes elders 16.12.1910.

[14] Bruno Gutmann, "Die gegenwärtige Lage der Dschaggamission", pp. 61-62.

[15] Minutes elders 8.9.1911.

based upon personal relationships covering all aspects of life and the whole life span.[16]

Gutmann's next aim was to introduce Christian customs to make up for the loss of many of the traditional customs either through the trend of times or through conversion to Christianity. This new set of customs was to sanctify everyday life and it was to stem from two sources, the Christian liturgical tradition and Chagga custom and culture.

In his essay on the state of the mission among the Chagga, Gutmann stated that another aim had to be the Africanization of personnel going beyond teacher training, and he suggests that former teachers should be employed as full time catechists and evangelists with the view of getting Africans to be trained as pastors at a time not too far ahead.[17]

To counteract the danger of Islam (and that of European civilization too) the church should go onto the offensive taking the Gospel down into the steppe, that means to the floating population there, to the soldiers, workers and traders at the government station, to the Muslims who had settled in the plains and to the Chagga moving downwards from the slopes of Mount Kilimanjaro.

When Gutmann took charge of Old Moshi congregation in 1910, this was not just a change in personnel, but it also meant a change in the concept of the congregation's work. This change did not come from within the congregation nor was it imposed by unavoidable circumstances, but the congregation was confronted with it by the new missionary who was a man with a strong personality.[18]

---

[16] Minutes elders Nov 1912.

[17] Several scholars have ascribed to Gutmann the view that he did not want ordination of African pastors. Bengt Sundkler writes: "Although boarding schools multiplied, Gutmann, the die-hard, would not accept the boarding school system on his station. He shunned it, as did teacher training and theological schools" (Bengt Sundkler and Christopher Steed, *A History of the Church in Africa*, Cambridge University Press, ²2001, p. 550). None of the three statements is true. Gutmann did not like boarding schools (Paul Fleisch, *Hundert Jahre lutherischer Mission*, p. 286), but the one at Moshi was closed already in 1907, three years before he came to Moshi. Gutmann wholeheartedly cooperated fully in the (admittedly slow) process of ordaining Tanzanian pastors, and when the new educational system with Marangu Teacher Training College at its hub and serious teaching of English included, was to be introduced he was one of the only three missionaries who voted in favour of it.

[18] When coming to Moshi in 1910, Gutmann was a missionary like others in the Leipzig Mission. During his work in Moshi he developed a distinct approach to missionary work which made him famous (and up to now much misunderstood). He wrote all his books in German. Several theses and books were written about him. In English see: Ernst Jaeschke, "Bruno Gutmann's Legacy", *Occasional Bulletin of Missionary Research*, October 1980; Martin F. Shao, *Bruno Gutmann's Missionary Method and its Influence on the Evangelical Lutheran Church in Tanzania Northern Diocese*, Erlangen: Verlag der Ev.-Luth. Mission, 1985; Ernst Jaeschke, *Gemeindeaufbau in Africa. Die Bedeutung Gutmann, Bruno's für das afri-*

What was new for the congregation in his concept? First of all a more positive attitude to Chagga society and culture. This was generally welcome but sometimes it was felt that he went too far. Secondly, he paid much less attention to the teachers, whose "European" attitudes presented to him a threat to the healthy development of the congregation. It is obvious that those concerned were not happy. The third new attitude for the Moshi Christians was his eagerness to develop new customs and rites and fourthly mention must be made of his eagerness to take the Gospel down into the steppe. It is obvious that the coming of Gutmann meant the strengthening of the beginning alliance of the church with traditional society and a loosening of its ties to the most progressive elements in Chagga society.

2. Gutmann's Background

To understand Bruno Gutmann and the impact he made on the congregation we have to know a little of his life history and of his Christian and social background. Gutmann came from a peasant family in Saxony in the eastern part of Germany, where Dresden and Leipzig were the major cities of the area. He became an orphan at the age of six. Because of this he experienced much mutual assistance in his extended family. He worked as a clerk with the town council until he felt the call to become a missionary. He entered the Leipzig Mission Seminary in 1895, where he got a thorough training in theology and languages (and also attended classes at the University of Leipzig in ethnography). He came to Kilimanjaro in 1902.[19]

Gutmann's cultural background is Romanticism, a cultural movement that reacted against the rationalism of the Enlightenment. It rediscovered the non-rational dimensions of life, thus making room for a renewed appreciation of both metaphysics and feeling.[20] Romanticism was also appreciative of the historical process and the differentiations it brought. So it rediscovered the value of tradition and of the cultural heritage transmitted from one generation to the other. Romanticism did not see the élite as the bearers of culture,

---

kanische Christentum, Stuttgart: Calwer Verlag, 1981; J.C. Winter, *Bruno Gutmann 1876-1966: a German Approach to Social Anthropology*, Oxford: 1979.

[19] For a sketch of his early years see: Bruno Gutmann, *Afrikaner - Europäer in nächstenschaftlicher Entsprechung. Gesammelte Aufsätze (ed. by Ernst Jaeschke)*, Stuttgart: Evangelisches Missionswerk, 1966.

[20] In Britain the ideas of Romanticism were first coherently formulated (though he did not use the term) by Edmund Burke (1729-1797) in his famous treatise "Reflections on the Revolution in France" (1790), published often after that, for example as: Edmund Burke, *Reflections on the Revolution in France*, Harmondsworth: Penguin, 1969.

but the ordinary people, the *Volk*.[21] With Romanticism also came a new wave of revival, the Great Awakening, which revived Protestant foreign missionary work after a period of serious decline, and led in 1836 to the founding of the Evangelical Lutheran Mission at Dresden, whose headquarters were later moved to Leipzig.[22]

3. Introducing New Christian Customs

Soon after his arrival Gutmann began to introduce new offices and new customs. The first attempt failed: He suggested that better care should be taken of the babies in Christian families (although with them infant mortality was far lower than with the rest of the population) and the best idea would be to follow the example of Mwika, where the wife of a teacher had been commissioned by the congregation to supervise childcare in Christian homesteads.[23] But this idea never caught on at Moshi.

About the same time it was discovered that a man from Machame had had sexual intercourse with women the day before they were to get married under the pretext of instructing them in preparation for marriage. To teach the bride before marriage was an old custom and this was now integrated into the church. The day before the wedding the couple and two elders or one elder and a married teacher would come together to the missionary who examined them whether they knew their catechism and especially the ten commandments. After this the elders who accompanied them could teach the couple.[24]

To make a Christian wedding more impressive he arranged that on a wedding day the church and the young couple's compound should be decorated, not just by a church official or just anyone—and this is typical for Gutmann—but by the members of the couple's age group. He also arranged

---

[21] *Volk* is difficult to translate into English. I often use folk, especially in composite terms like folkhood and folk church. Folk in English often implies the meaning of "ordinary folk", and that seems to me to be quite appropriate.

[22] Gustav Warneck, *Abriß einer Geschichte der protestantischen Missionen von der Reformation bis auf die Gegenwart*, Berlin: Martin Warneck, 1910, p. 141.

[23] Minutes elders 23.9.1910.

[24] Minutes elders 14.10.1910. For details see "Brautexamen am Kilimandscharo" in Bruno Gutmann, *Afrikaner - Europäer in nächstenschaftlicher Entsprechung. Gesammelte Aufsätze (ed. by Ernst Jaeschke)*, Stuttgart: Evangelisches Missionswerk, 1966, pp. 192-196, originally published as: Bruno Gutmann, "Brautexamen am Kilimandscharo", in *Deutscher evangelischer Missions-Kalender* 10, 1935, pp. 28-30).

that after the church ceremony the couple would be accompanied to their compound, this "being opened" by hymns, psalm reading and prayer.[25]

Gutmann also arranged that the Sunday after the death of a Christian a memorial hymn should be sung. This would be sung without harmonium and the relatives were allowed to inform the pastor on Saturday which hymn they would like.[26]

Soon another new custom was introduced which still exists in at least some of the Old Moshi parishes, the baptism anniversary.[27] This meant, and means until today, that during morning prayers the names of those who had been baptized on that date in one of the previous years were read out. Special mention was made of those having died or lapsed. Then prayers were offered for those baptized on that day and at the end all would sing a hymn standing, if possible that of their baptismal class.[28]

When Gutmann introduced these new customs (and it was Gutmann who introduced them, although he discussed everything properly in the elders' meetings), he did not meet with any opposition and this is understandable, as they did not involve any major changes. But with other innovations Gutmann did meet opposition. On 28.6.1912 he informed the elders[29] that during the folk festival after the conference of all Chagga congregations he intended to produce several Chagga children's games in order that they should not be forgotten.[30] Very quickly he met with strong opposition from the teachers with whom he had a long discussion on 7.8.1912. They related that the people would not like the children to play at school; they should be brought up to work. If they played at school they would play on their way home and then delay to take the goats to the pastures. This would decrease the influence of the school in the homes. Gutmann realized that the teachers shared very strongly this public opinion. So he gave in, accepting that to strengthen the influence of the school must remain the most important aim. Thus he dropped his proposal for the time being, but he still hoped to produce at least one game. Yet in the elders' meeting 23.8.1912 he dared to mention his plan again, but this time the elders agreed very much and even suggested games for themselves. The agreement of the elders was much facilitated by the

---

[25] Minutes elders 14.10.1910.
[26] Minutes elders 14.10.1910.
[27] Minutes elders 16.12.1910.
[28] Bruno Gutmann, "Die gegenwärtige Lage der Dschaggamission", pp. 61-62.
[29] Minutes elders 28.6.1912.
[30] Minutes elders 28.6.1912.

argument that such games would strengthen the children: for the same reason also Chief Rindi had ordered such games to be played.[31]

4. Revitalizing the Clan Structure

For the "new" old games, opposition had come from the progressive quarter represented by the teachers. A different kind of opposition Gutmann met when he tried to strengthen the clan. The Chagga had been organized all the years of their existence into clans, that is groups of people all claiming descent from one common founder father. The clan was the first political organization of the Chagga, as formerly every clan had a settlement area of its own. With the rise of territorial chieftainships the clans lost somewhat in importance, but still played am important role as they were the units of mutual assistance and mutual obligation. Many clans began to grow and also to spread, thus reducing the meaning of clan sometimes to not much more than a common name.[32] Around 1910 many clans had already lost their organization, they had no clan head and no meetings any more. For many Chagga the clan seemed to be no longer an expedient means of social organization, thus they did not any longer care much for it. But for Gutmann the clan was not a matter of social expediency, it was a primal tie, which means a divine order, unchangeable because it was part of the image of God in which man was created. Thus for Gutmann the church was obliged to fight to preserve this order. This Gutmann did wholeheartedly, but not very successfully. He tried to open the eyes of the congregation for the values of the clan. After several brief references to the value of the clan for the church Gutmann on the 28.6.1912 delivered a long lecture to the elders on this topic.[33] Here are the main points:

1. The clan gives mutual help, supervision and guidance.
2. It is the clan structure that up to now safeguarded the existence of the Chagga as an ethnic group.
3. The clan has prepared the Chagga for the acceptance of the Gospel.
4. All these gifts of God in the clan structure must be preserved.
5. Therefore we have to organize the clan anew in Christian understanding.

---

[31] Minutes elders 23.8.1912.
[32] Even now, a Chagga must not marry someone with the same name, even if the common ancestor may have lived several generations ago.
[33] Minutes elders 28.6.1912.

6. If this is being done the clan will do many jobs, which up to now the church has to look after.
6. Practical steps to reach this aim are: clan-meetings, communal fieldwork, writing down of clan and lineage histories.

After this lecture the elders promised their cooperation in an attempt to influence the congregation. But they declared that this great work could not be brought to completion within one generation. Gutmann replied: The more it is necessary to lay a firm foundation!

Here the elders saw reality more clearly, because their remark is open to another interpretation, taking what they expressed in terms of future times as meaning that *now* the response would be very partial indeed. But response there was. In June 1914 the first Christian clan meeting took place (of the Olotu clan, from which Zakayo Olotu, the church elder of Tsunduny came), including common attendance at the Sunday service and an offering for the church building fund.[34] Gutmann took this opportunity to encourage the clans to write down their histories and traditions as the basis for a clan book, and for clans that had lost their organization; Gutmann suggested that as soon as the Christian part of the clan would be strong enough, that they should start holding clan meetings.

With his plans to reactivate the clans Gutmann never got far. True, some shared his concern to some extent for example Yohane Kimambo,[35] but as a whole, the elders agreed only reluctantly, and this was, as it often is, the most efficient opposition. Why did Gutmann not meet with more response? Was the clan not an old Chagga institution? Definitely, but Chagga society was in change, and Gutmann tried to halt this change at a certain point. But people did not like to be turned backwards.

5. Agricultural Supervisors

One of the most far-reaching innovations that Gutmann introduced was the office of agricultural supervisor. Gutmann felt that a number of Christians did not work hard enough in their fields and did not keep their domestic animals properly. He discussed this problem with the elders. It is not recorded whether the elders agreed that some of the Christians were lazy, but it was clear that both agriculture and animal husbandry could be improved.

---

[34] Minutes elders 28.6.1912; cf Bruno Gutmann, *Das Dschaggaland und seine Christen*, Leipzig: Verlag der Evang.-Luth. Mission, 1925, pp. 122-123. The Olotu clan monument can still be seen today.

[35] See Gutmann's report on a lesson of his on the value of the clan in Bruno Gutmann, "Afrikanische Charakterköpfe", pp. 50-52. (60).

The area of Moshi was not fertile, and often not enough food was produced,[36] and around 1910 there had been several particularly bad years. Gutmann got the elders to agree to the plan to choose agricultural supervisors. In April 1911 for every *mtaa* one supervisor was chosen. They were: Luka for Mowo, Georgi for Mdavi, Zakaria Ringo, teacher, for Shia, Gabrieli Maro, church elder, for Sangu, Zakayo Olotu, church elder, for Mahoma, Yonatan for Tela and Yohane for Mbokomu.[37] Their task was to see especially that the Christians looked after their fields in the plains properly. Their office continued to exist even after Gutmann had left, only to be dropped when the independence government introduced the office of "Bwana Shamba".

Although the Christians themselves had elected these agricultural supervisors, a year later they still complained that the majority of the Christians had not accepted their office yet.[38] It is also clear that sometimes the agricultural supervisors neglected their duties.

6. The Great Harvest Festival

The office of agricultural supervisor had no roots in the old. The contrary is true of one of the most cherished customs of the congregation, the great harvest festival that was introduced in 1911. It takes place after finishing the maize harvest and the first was held on the 24.9.1911.[39] This day was to be a Christian festival for everyone, with gift offerings, a thanksgiving service, games for the children and, as the main feature, the *mtingo* dance, the traditional harvest dance, which at that time had fallen almost into oblivion and was "rediscovered" by Gutmann.[40]

The first festival was a success, and it became an established custom. Harvest festivals were celebrated also in other congregations, but nowhere it seems to have taken root so deeply in Chagga life. Why? The main feature distinguishing the harvest festival at Moshi from that at other places was the traditional *mtingo* dance, the dance that Gutmann had christianized by caring that the texts of the songs should be clearly related to God, the creator. It was this dance and the atmosphere it created that made the festival so attractive all through the years.

---

[36] Kathleen Stahl states that only under Chief Abraham Moshi began to produce enough food.
[37] It is not clear, why no mention is made of Kidia.
[38] Minutes elders 12.4.1912.
[39] Minutes elders 8.9.1911.
[40] Bruno Gutmann, *Gemeindeaufbau aus dem Evangelium*, pp. 97-98 describes the great harvest festival in some detail.

7. Sunday Afternoon Dances

During the next years Gutmann introduced many more new customs and institutions, but only one is to be mentioned here, one that always remained a controversial one, among the missionaries but even within the congregation. Gutmann had realized that Sunday was a day of danger for the youths (actually not only for them) and that they needed proper entertainment.[41] Therefore he revived the old dances and integrated them into the church by making the Christian age group leaders (there was one in every *mtaa*) responsible to the church elders. The dancing grounds were chosen by the church and supervised by elder Christians acting as dancing ground supervisors.

8. Opposition to the Cultural Approach

During these four years Gutmann had reached his aim of organizing the church more fully and to do this in strong relationship to traditional order and values. About this development the teachers were not happy, and friction arose between them and the "ordinary" Christians. On 22.7.1914 Gutmann called a meeting of all elders, teachers and agricultural supervisors because the teachers were said to have held the opinion that they were not sufficiently being consulted. And the teachers were accused of feeling too proud to attend the Christians' meetings and other meeting of the church-organs. Gutmann opened the discussion, but to his regret no discussion took place on the difference between the teachers and the other leaders. The result was that a new institution was created, the *mtaa* council (which should coordinate the work of the church in any given *mtaa*). These meetings were to take place once a month and were open to everyone, but every agent of the church was expected to attend regularly.[42] There is no sign that this new institution answered any real need and very often the meetings did not take place and for sure it did not solve the problem of the teachers. Here is one point where Gutmann's attempts to root the church as much as possible in the old began to estrange the progressive elements of the church.

Here it may be the place to relate a little episode, which shows that what for Gutmann, and his fellow Europeans was a successful way of rooting the church in the old, for the Africans concerned was seen as a completely new thing. In 1911 Gutmann had to build a church at Sangu (where Gabrieli Maro was church elder) and he choose to build it in the way of the traditional

---

[41] The elders said the youth walk around the *mtaa* to find a place where they can get beer. All sexes and age-group meet there.
[42] Minutes elders 22.7.1974.

Chagga houses. But that would not have been large enough, so he enlarged it to have a diameter of 11 m, and he build it as if he would put a second circular house on top of the first. This Paul Fleisch in his history of the Leipzig Mission describes as related organically to the way of life of the Chagga.[43] Ndesanjo Kitange, who helped to erect this church, said: "We had never seen such a thing."[44]

There was opposition still from another side: On the mission lived a deaconess, Berta Schulz, who cared for orphaned children and who taught Swahili and German in the evenings to the pupils living at or near the mission, something Gutmann disapproved of completely, especially the teaching of German.[45]

9. The Cultural Approach Firmly Established

The atmosphere in the elders' meetings was generally an atmosphere of full cooperation. But it is clear that Gutmann was the source of all important inspirations. All innovations, except that to go around from homestead to homestead singing at advent time,[46] were Gutmann's ideas. Some quotations may show this kind of cooperation: "I develop the plan of a harvest festival".[47] "I show to the elders the value of the (children's) games".[48] "Then I discuss with the elders the fact that this year the people do not want to cultivate".[49] These are just to mention a few examples. But Gutmann, though a strong personality, was by no means a dictator who simply pushed through the things he wanted. He asked for the approval of the elders, who sometimes refused. In other cases the elders demanded first to be given opportunity to talk things over with the congregation in the *mitaa*. Also it seems that the elders were more willing to agree to a thing during the meetings than to implement it when at home in their *mitaa*. Gutmann is being remembered for being *kali* (harsh) sometimes but not for pushing through what he wanted in the elder's meetings. But he did not get tired quickly as the example of the children's games shows.

During the years of 1910-1914 Gutmann definitely left his mark on the Moshi congregation. He was able to organize the congregation according to

---

[43] Paul Fleisch, *Hundert Jahre lutherischer Mission*, p. 305.
[44] Interview Ndesanjo Kitange 27.5.1971.
[45] Interview Nahori Malisa 25.5.1971.
[46] This the Christians started on their own account (Minutes elders 5.12.1913).
[47] Minutes elders 8.9.1911.
[48] Minutes elders 28.6.1912.
[49] Minutes elders 6.12.1913.

the lines he had envisaged and he introduced customs and offices that are still in existence or have at least survived his return to Germany in 1938 for many years. Gutmann did his work against a background of disappointment and desperation. When he came to Moshi there was a time of depression. Moshi had been completely subdued. The Germans had hanged their chief and Moshi had lost its paramountcy.[50] Now Moshi was down, people were disheartened, they had lost faith in themselves, many did not even want to work their fields. In this situation Gutmann tried to give them back their hearts. This he did by reminding them of their past glories under Rindi,[51] by collecting their traditions and customs and also by making his people work hard and cultivate enough, and it seems that this attempt is in fact the deepest root of the institution of the agricultural supervisor, of his tree and fountain sermon on the eve of the harvest festival, of his non religious reforestation schemes as well as of his religious ones (planting two trees each year at the fountain during the tree and fountain sermon, and the children's valley where the confirmands planted their trees).

In the years after 1910 Moshi did recover, and in this recovery Gutmann played his part, and as far as church history is concerned, it is no overstatement to say that he was the most important event in the years of 1910 to 1916.

---

[50] There had never been a paramount chief among the Chagga, but when the Europeans arrived, some chiefs were trying to gain supremacy, and Rindi was regarded by most travellers as some kind of a paramount.

[51] See Bruno Gutmann, *Häuptling Rindi von Moshi - Ein Afrikanisches Helden - und Herrscherleben*, Köln, n.d. (1928).

The Congregation During the First World War

1. Effects of The War on the Congregation

When the First World War broke out in Europe, Germany had only weak forces in Tanzania, but unfortunately for the population of East Africa these forces had a most able commander, von Lettow-Vorbeck, who managed to keep the British and Allied Forces out of Tanzania until 1916 and to keep on fighting until the armistice in Europe made him surrender in 1918 in Zambia.[1] But this he managed at the cost of enormous losses of African lives, not so much among the soldiers but among the carrier corps on both sides. Here are two examples of how the war affected the congregation: When a British attack on Moshi became imminent, the local population had to make a big clearing below the government station so that the defenders could see the British troops when attacking the government station. This work had to be done on a Sunday. The Christians of Old Moshi were in church and after the service soldiers came to take them to the government station by force. There they were beaten thoroughly[2] and chained and ordered to work for three months. On Monday Gutmann went down to talk to the commander who agreed that they should not work in chains, that they should be allowed to be brought their food from home and that they should work for three weeks instead of three months, and Gutmann stressed that it being a Sunday, they had done nothing wrong.[3]

The second example is that of a seminary trained teacher, Nderangusho Maro of Mowo. He was made to be a 'boy' of the German soldiers, they took him to Pare where he deserted "his" troops and tried to find refuge with Fuchs, Superintendent of the Leipzig Mission. Fuchs returned him to the German troops where he was beaten badly and died.[4]

These were not the only losses. Other teachers who had been trained at Marangu over the years took up other work.[5] Many Christians were conscripted as carriers and a number of them never returned. In 1917 the chief

---

[1] Zambia honoured him in 1996 by a special stamp in the National Monuments Series, which also features the Livingstone Monument and Mbereshi Mission.
[2] There are rumours that their cries were even heard as far uphill as Kidia. (remark Esau Malisa, 22.5.1971).
[3] Interview Nahori Malisa 25.5.1971.
[4] Interview Ndesanjo Kitange 27.5.1971.
[5] Interview Ndesanjo Kitange 27.5.1971.

of Moshi, together with eight other Chagga chiefs, due to material largely provided by Catholic missionaries,[6] was found guilty of treason and exiled. After a year all of them were found not guilty and the chief of Moshi was restored his previous office.[7]

How did the church live and develop during those troubled years? Any assessment must be made on the background of events in other congregations of the Leipzig Mission. During the years of 1914 and 1915 the church everywhere grew as before the war, but in 1916 there was a definite slowdown and a revival of traditional religion. In some congregations considerable numbers left the church, including some of the leaders. Even anti-Christian riots occurred.[8]

How do events at Old Moshi compare with this? All through the war, the work of the congregation continued as usual. Even the day when Gutmann was taken to Moshi to be interned in 1916, baptismal instruction took place as usual, and all through the war not a single service was delayed[9] and school work was continued although the teachers got hardly any remuneration, and the church grew considerably in numbers. While within the four years 1910-1913 only 223 people had been baptized, for the two years 1914-1915 there were 394 baptisms, and during the next two years (1916-1917) the number of baptisms was 362.[10] How can this difference be explained? A casual answer might be: This is no wonder because the missionary was there all through the war. Sure, the fact that Gutmann refused to withdraw with the German troops and after the occupation was taken away from Old Moshi for only three days (18-20.3.1916) did help in the work of the congregation.[11] But this is only a partial answer. There was for example considerable trouble at Masama, which also had a missionary all the years.[12] The full answer is that Christianity had really taken root in Old Moshi. This is illustrated by a little episode involving a young Christian herd boy, which occurred when Gutmann had been taken to Moshi to be interned. A grown up man told the boy: "You must become a pagan again like I am, because they have taken the missionary prisoner and they won't let him return." The boy answered:

---

[6] For a treatment of both Catholic and Lutheran missionary work on Kilimanjaro from today's perspective see: Bengt Sundkler and Christopher Steed, *A History of the Church in Africa*, Cambridge University Press, ²2001, p. 546-551.
[7] Bruno Gutmann, *Gemeindeaufbau aus dem Evangelium*, p. 184.
[8] Paul Fleisch, *Hundert Jahre lutherischer Mission*, pp. 347-350.
[9] Bruno Gutmann, *Das Dschaggaland und seine Christen*, p. 37.
[10] Baptism register Moshi 1910ff.
[11] Interview Nahori Malisa 25.5.1971, Bruno Gutmann, *Das Dschaggaland und seine Christen* p. 172 and Paul Fleisch, *Hundert Jahre lutherischer Mission,* p. 344.
[12] Paul Fleisch, *Hundert Jahre lutherischer Mission,* p. 347.

"Should have happened what I have not heard of, that God has been put into prison as well?" The same was expressed in a more sophisticated way by Zakayo Olotu of Tsunduny, one of the church elders who said: "Now we believe because we have realized ourselves that Jesus is the Christ, the saviour also of our nation."[13]

What also helped was the fact that the congregation was big and comprised a considerable percentage of the population, at least in Old Moshi chiefdom. Another very important factor is that Old Moshi congregation had a considerable number of leaders who were able to work independently, and this they proved after the war when Gutmann was repatriated to Germany. Before coming to that period, mention must be made of New Moshi.

2. The Growth of New Moshi and the Move of the Government Station thereto

Another event that did not have to do much with the war is very important for that time: The growth of New Moshi town. When the railway reached Kilimanjaro in 1912 its railhead was not in the mountainous region of the Chagga, but in the plains below Old Moshi. Soon the railway station grew into a town, symbolizing that now everything was of a larger scale, and that the centre of Uchagga would now lie outside the inter-chiefdom rivalries of former days. The new town became to be of particular influence for Old Moshi as it was within easy walking distance, bringing into Old Moshi many new forces for good and bad.

As long as the Germans ruled, the government station remained at Old Moshi. The British transferred it to New Moshi in 1919.[14] Gutmann was never very fond of New Moshi, but he saw the congregation's responsibility for missionary work there in the same way, as he had felt obliged to work at the government station at Old Moshi. In 1919 Anton Tarimo started schoolwork there together with evangelistic activity.[15] In 1920 the first non-Chagga there were receiving baptismal instruction.[16] They were taught at New Moshi and had their Sunday services there. These two facts were foreshadowing that New Moshi would become independent of Old Moshi soon. And as a matter of fact the work at New Moshi had not been started as an outpost of Old Moshi (like places as Mbokomu, Sangu, Tela etc) but as missionary

---

[13] Bruno Gutmann, *Das Dschaggaland und seine Christen*, p. 6.
[14] Kathleen M. Stahl, *History of the Chagga People of Kilimanjaro*, London 1964, pp. 274–278.
[15] Bruno Gutmann, *Anton Tarimo, der Evangelist von Moshi*, Leipzig: Verlag der Evang.-Luth. Mission, 1924, p. 16.
[16] It seems as if the first baptism of 14 adults took place only in 1924 (baptism register).

work (like Kahe and Okuma). There had already been a missionary at New Moshi in 1914 who reported to Gutmann that the work was getting on well and that a chapel would be build soon.[17] But this work was brought to a standstill due to the war.

---

[17] The German personnel at the government station had already donated 115 Rupies (letter of the missionary of New Moshi to Gutmann, 24.4.1914).

The Congregation under the Leadership of Filipo Njau and Yohane Kimambo

The year 1919 saw the situation in church and nation getting almost back to normal. The travel restrictions for the German missionaries were more and more relaxed, and they got on well with the British administration. But their destiny was to be decided no longer in East Africa, as Smuts had decided it in 1916.[1]

1. Gutmann Hands over to Filipo Njau and Yohane Kimambo

When the mission began to face the probability that all German missionaries would have to leave,[2] the idea of ordaining African pastors was discussed: But they decided against it as premature, a decision that Gutmann describes with the words: they resisted the temptation.[3] Thus when Gutmann had to leave, he had to hand over the congregation to unordained leaders. Two experienced teachers were chosen as caretakers. For Mbokomu Yohane Kimambo was the choice. He was among the first group of teachers who had got a seminary training, after which he taught and lived at Kidia for more than ten years, after which he retired to Mbokomu due to insufficient health. He was at Mbokomu when he was chosen to be one of the leaders. The second who was chosen was Filipo Njau. He was from Kidia and his clan was small, but important people came from it, for example Elisa Njau,[4] the elder brother of Filipo Njau, who was church elder for a long time and Petro Njau, his younger brother,[5] founder of the famous coffee cooperative KNCU (Kilimanjaro Native Cooperative Union).[6] Filipo Njau was not a mission child like Yohane Kimambo and Anton Tarimo and Imanuel Mkony; he lived at home while attending the mission school. He was on the first teachers to be trained at Marangu instead of at Moshi. He spoke quite a good German,

---

[1] When Smuts realized that Gutmann had been detained, he ordered his release with the words: "I am not at war with missionaries!" (Paul Fleisch, *Hundert Jahre lutherischer Mission*, p. 344).
[2] A book very useful to appreciate the atmosphere and the working style that made such decisions possible is: Harold Nicolson, *Peacemaking 1919*, revised edition 1943, reprinted 1967 (London).
[3] Bruno Gutmann, *Unter dem Trutzbaum*, p. 41.
[4] For example: Bruno Gutmann, *Unter dem Trutzbaum* 41.
[5] Bruno Gutmann, Afrikanische Charakterköpfe, p. 44.
[6] Suzan Geiger Rogers, The Search for Political Focus on Kilimanjaro: A History of Chagga Politics, 1916-1952, with Special Reference to the Cooperative Movement and Indirect Rule, PhD Dar es Salaam, 1972.

fluent Swahili and knew English as well. Yohane Kimambo and Filipo Njau were equals, Filipo Njau working mainly at Moshi and Yohane Kimambo mainly at Mbokomu, but Filipo Njau was the leader of the congregation as a whole and the stronger personality.

2. The Work of the Caretakers

The last Sunday before Gutmann actually left (8.8.1920), Yohane Kimambo and Filipo Njau were ordained for their work.[7] They were not ordained in the technical meaning of the word, but were entrusted with leading the services and with the pastoral care of the congregation. They had to promise to do their work according to Luther's Catechism and the Confessio Augustana and to be part of the congregation and its organs. To express this more clearly, not Filipo Njau, but a church elder became chairman of the elders' meeting.[8] Filipo Njau and Yohane Kimambo were called caretakers (*Gemeindepfleger*). But as a matter of fact they were the pastors in charge of the congregation, and they did the work that Gutmann had done. And they did it quite well. To this all agree, and Gutmann in his writings is full of praise for these two leaders.

They had to care for a large and growing congregation. When they took over the leadership of the congregation, there were twelve schools and that meant at least as many preaching places. The centre of the congregation was Kidia, where every Sunday about 400 people attended, and other important places were Mbokomu with 150 and Tela with 100 attendants on an average Sunday. It is interesting to note that Shia, later to become the centre of a parish as well, had only an attendance of 25, the reason being that it was situated more down hill, where the missionary work reached later.

On the 1.11.1920 Moshi congregation had 1523 members, of them in Moshi chieftaincy 1359, in Mbokomu 164 and 7 in Moshi Town and until Gutmann left, the overall membership had increased to 1629.[9] This gives a rough percentage of Christians for Moshi of 20%, Mbokomu of 7%, New Moshi less than 11%. Although counting only 20% of the population at Moshi, the Christians were the strongest force in society and even the chief was contemplating conversion.[10] There were no rivals.[11] Islam had lost its

---

[7] Kidia church announcements 10.8.1920.
[8] Bruno Gutmann, *Gemeindeaufbau aus dem Evangelium*.
[9] Statistics of the Congregation 1.1.1920.
[10] Bruno Gutmann, *Das Dschaggaland und seine Christen*, p. 72.
[11] Except in New Moshi.

aggressiveness, the Catholic mission did not work in Old Moshi, and resistance of traditional religion was growing weaker.

3. Scarcity of the Sacraments

The life of the congregation continued along the same lines as before the war, even at Christmas the church was decorated as usual. But there was one setback for the congregation. There was no one to administer the sacraments of baptism (except to a person in extremis) and Holy Communion. And there was no one to perform Christian marriages. Filipo Njau and Yohane Kimambo were permitted to give all the necessary instructions for baptism, they were authorized to prepare people to partake in Holy Communion, they even "taught marriage", but for baptism, communion and marriage the people had to wait for an ordained pastor to come. When the missionaries had to leave due to the Versailles treaty,[12] one of them, Eisenschmidt, was allowed to stay because he was considered to be of Russian nationality, though he was an ethnic German. He managed to distribute the sacraments to all Christians. This was made possible by the Lutheran practice there at that time to have communion only about four times a year and only in the parish church, and adult baptism took place anyhow only once a year, and for newborn children it did not matter much to wait because in case of emergency they would be baptized by the caretaker, by a teacher[13] or by any Christian around. Thus the church lost the opportunity to rethink its theology of the ministry and also there was not much need to think of ordaining African pastors, as the caretakers there provided pastoral care and the sacraments were provided by Eisenschmidt. What seems to have troubled the people more than that their half-pastors[14] could not dispense communion and baptism was the fact that also weddings had to be delayed until the day when the pastor came?[15] Nahori Malisa remembers with gratitude that his marriage

---

[12] The Versailles peace treaty included the provision that from Tanzania and other former colonies, German nationals and missions would be excluded for a period of five years.
[13] See baptism register of those years. Imanuel Mkony baptized several children in those years.
[14] This term is used to show that in reality they were pastors although they did not have the full pastor's rights (I got the idea of using this term following the use of the term half-bishop in E.A. Ayandele, *The Missionary Impact on Modern Nigeria 1842-1994*, London, 1966, cf. p. 233).
[15] In Lutheran theology marriage is not a sacrament, but in practice it is treated like the highest sacrament. A little incident on this: When in the 1970s in the Lutheran Church on Mt Kilimanjaro it was decided to allow certain evangelists ("wainjilisti wa Sinodi") to administer the sacraments, they differed from the ordained pastors (wachungaji) only in the fact that they were not allowed to conduct weddings. This differentiation was ecclesiastical, not civil. The government of Tanzania did not require ordination for a marriage officer. In the Kanisa la Biblia, where I worked at that time, most of the marriage officers were not ordained.

was the last one celebrated by Gutmann before he left.[16] And which couple likes to be married on the same day and in the same church as six other couples?[17]

4. Scarcity of Money

Another problem arose in schoolwork. There was no longer money to pay the teachers.[18] Quite a number of them went on to teach,[19] but others left their jobs, some of them to return as soon as money came into sight again.[20] But the general picture was encouraging. One teacher told me: "All work continued. It grew in strength, without salary."[21] But money was a problem, and on the 19.1.1921 it was decided that no one who had not paid his church tax for three years could partake in Holy Communion, because "he does not like work with us."[22] But on 16.10.1921 they were allowed to partake in the communion of Advent 1921,[23] but not further without paying.[24] And the church income showed indeed a marked increase.

The collection of church taxes was:[25].

1919	580.00 sh[26]
1920	264.00 sh[27] the year Gutmann left.
1921	580.00 sh[28] the year of the above decision
1922	694.50 sh
1923	754.50 sh
1924	
1925	976.50 sh.[29]

---

[16] Interview Nahori Malisa 25.5.1971.
[17] For ex: On 31.3.1921 there were seven marriages performed by Eisenschmidt at Old Moshi. When Ndesanjo Kitange married, they were three couples (Interview Ndesanjo Kitange 27.5.1971) On the 8.12.1920 there were 13 couples (baptism register 1920, 1921).
[18] For three years (Interview Ndesanjo Kitange 27.5.1971), for about two years (Minutes elders 16.8.1922), but after that they got very little per month at first.
[19] Interview Nahori Malisa 25.5.1971.
[20] On the 26.5.1922 it was decided to give every teacher 2 Rupies per month, and on 16.8.1922 two teachers were discussed who wanted to return to their jobs (minutes elders).
[21] Interview Nahori Malisa 25.5.1971.
[22] Minutes elders 19.1.1921 (At that time the elders' minutes were kept in Swahili).
[23] Minutes elders 16.10.1921. This law was kept in force all the time, whereas the law forbidding circumcision was lifted as having no biblical foundation. But had this one?
[24] Minutes elders 18.8.1920.
[25] Statistical returns in the minutes book of the elders' meeting.
[26] At that time the currency was still the Rupee which later was to be exchanged at the rate of 1 Rupee to 2 shillings.
[27] Statistical returns in the minutes book of the elders' meeting.
[28] Ibid.

The economic recovery after the war is not a sufficient explanation of the rising church income. It must be due partly to a growing understanding of responsibility. Not only income increased, but also church-membership. When Gutmann left, the congregation had 1627 members, in 1923 it had 1844.[30] The numbers of adult baptisms were:

1920   69
1922   65
1923   44
1924   53
1925   189.[31]

It is true that numbers and money is not a sufficient indicator for the spiritual development of a congregation, but these facts are supplemented by what people say. Another point indicating that the life of the congregation developed along healthy lines was in 1921 the decision of the congregation to start the extension of the church building which had become to small. Some preliminary work had been done before the war, but now the congregation started it on their own initiative. It was finished in 1923.[32]

5. American Missionaries at Old Moshi

When the Leipzig missionaries had to leave, it was first supposed that the Lutheran Iowa Mission should take care of the "orphaned mission", and thus Zeilinger, missionary of Iowa, went to Tanzania in June 1922.[33] But afterwards it became clear that Iowa could not meet the British conditions and so the equally Lutheran Augustana Mission was given the responsibility for the work, Hult being their leader. Both leaders resided at Moshi, Zeilinger March 1922-1925 until his furlough (he worked for Augustana then) and Hult 1925-1926.[34] In addition to them, Dr. Anderson and Elveda Bonanda (nurse) stayed at Old Moshi 1923 - February 1926.[35]

What was the effect of the coming of the Americans to Moshi? They seem to have brought some improvements in the material standards of the congregation. But there is another side to it: What did Zeilinger's coming

---

[29] Report of Income and Disbursements of the Moshi Congregation for the year 1925. (in baptism register book).
[30] Statistical returns in the minutes book of the elders meetings.
[31] Baptism register.
[32] Bruno Gutmann, *Das Dschaggaland und seine Christen*, pp. 110-112 '"Sie erweitern ihre Kirche".
[33] Paul Fleisch, *Hundert Jahre lutherischer Mission*, p. 354.
[34] Paul Fleisch, *Hundert Jahre lutherischer Mission*, pp. 354-357.
[35] On the American interlude see: Paul Fleisch, *Hundert Jahre lutherischer Mission*, pp. 353-364.

mean for the spiritual life of the congregation? Here it is important to hear the voice of the church-members. In talking with them, the names of Zeilinger and Hult were often mentioned, but just as facts. There was hardly any colour in the speech when they were mentioned. They do not seem to have had any strong influence on the congregation. Asking more deeply, it became clear that they did not understand much of the life of the people, they were just guests.[36] Ndesanjo Kitange stresses that spiritually they were of no difference, but otherwise.[37] They remained strangers, and so they were not blamed that they did not understand many things.[38] Maybe Zeilinger felt this somehow when on 2.1.1924 he decided that Filipo Njau should continue writing the minutes of the elders' meetings, and that this should be in Chagga, not in a foreign language.[39] It is also important to note that after Gutmann's return there are three entries in the minutes book blaming the Americans for baptizing people who should not have been baptized[40] without further consultation and for granting absolution without looking into the matter properly.[41] Definitely they were not conversant with the life of the Chagga. Was it the right decision to place the Americans at Moshi? Most probably not. When Zeilinger came to Moshi, it was one of the most flourishing congregations on Kilimanjaro, growing able leaders. It was well organized, large and healthy. Other congregations with a considerable amount of backsliders, with a revival of traditional religion, trouble among the local leaders etc. were left without a missionary. I think that in such congregations missionaries should have been placed more urgently. And for the more advanced congregations regular visits would have been sufficient. This would perhaps have made the leadership of Filipo Njau (and not of him alone) to develop into full pastoral care.

This transfer of power was transacted without consultation of the Africans concerned. Leipzig tried to hand over to Iowa, failing this, to Augustana. And in the end Augustana returned the work to Leipzig.[42] The Africans at Old Moshi were happy when the Germans returned, after all they had not asked the Americans to come and they preferred the Germans because they had got used to their ways and the Germans in general and Gutmann especially had a considerable understanding for the Chagga. This all was done

---

[36] Interview Nahori Malisa 25.5.1971.
[37] Interview Ndesanjo Kitange 27.5.1971.
[38] Interview Petro Moshi (Ex-Mangi).
[39] Entry by Zeilinger in elders' minutes.
[40] Minutes elders 7.7.1926, 7.3.1933.
[41] Minutes elders 6.3.1929.
[42] Paul Fleisch, *Hundert Jahre lutherischer Mission*, p. 359.

without consultation, although Gutmann defended against Augustana what he knew was the African standpoint when he told the Augustana missionaries: Do not split Kilimanjaro, it is contrary to what the African Christians want, only to get the reply by Anderson that in this matter the Chagga Christians had no say.[43]

6. The Circumcision Controversy

For the years of 1923 – 1926 the dominating event in Old Moshi congregation was the circumcision controversy. Its origin was outside the congregation. On 12 and 13.3.1922 there was a church elders' meeting at Machame which discussed the issue of circumcision.[44] At this meeting circumcision was not forbidden, but it was reported to Old Moshi that children should decide for themselves after confirmation. The elders decided that the matter should be discussed in the *mitaa*.[45] Nobody seems to have taken the matter seriously; twice it was put on the agenda and not discussed.[46] On 13.9.1922 it was decided that Filipo Njau should write down everything so that it might be discussed in the *mitaa* under the leadership of the elders and the teachers. The results of the discussion should be brought before a meeting of the elders and the teachers.[47] Again, matters developed slowly. Only on 18.7.1923 the elders discussed the matter again, deciding that children under instruction for confirmation should not be circumcised, so that they might decide for themselves afterwards.[48] Before this date however, there had been a teachers' and elders' meeting in January 1923 of the whole church that had decided to abolish circumcision completely.[49] I could not find any explanation for the time lag, but in August 1923 in Old Moshi the issue began to heat up. On 15.8.1923 Zeilinger was asked for his judgment. He informed the elders that the local Christians would have to decide for themselves, and if they agreed among themselves that circumcision was bad, he as pastor would help them "to remove this trouble".[50] And on 5.9.1923 the elders' meeting decided that no one should be circumcised anymore.[51] This decision was unanimous, but only technically so. Those who decided were the elders under the leadership

---

[43] Paul Fleisch, *Hundert Jahre lutherischer Mission*, p 359.
[44] Minutes elders 22.3.1922.
[45] Minutes elders 23.3.1922.
[46] Minutes elders 22.3. 1922; 10.5.1922.
[47] Minutes elders 13.9.1922.
[48] Minutes elders 18.7.1923.
[49] Paul Fleisch, *Hundert Jahre lutherischer Mission*, p. 417.
[50] Minutes elders 15.8.1923.
[51] Minutes elders 5.9.1923.

of two teachers, and the big majority of the Christians were against this decision. But not only they, even many elders did not like it. There was a large tacit opposition. Those who were against circumcision stressed two points:

1. God has created man in his image. He did not make any mistake, so it is wrong to "improve" his creation by circumcision.
2. It is painful and not necessary.[52]

Those who supported the decision were the more "progressive" people,[53] mostly seminary trained teachers. Especially mentioned were Yohane Kimambo, Oforo Lyatoo, teacher of Tela-Oru[54] and the father of Rev. Elinsa Kisaka.[55] Outside support came mainly from Machame,[56] the chiefdom with the shortest history, populated from other chiefdoms, where only the chiefly clan remembers its origin, and also from Pare,[57] where the percentage of Christians was much smaller and from those who had been to the seminary at Marangu.

Most of the elders seem to have agreed only under a certain pressure, for example Gabrieli Maro of Sangu,[58] who had brought up the matter for discussion in 1910 for the first time. And almost everyone else was against it. They felt it to be "a hard law not liked by the Christians",[59] and that Filipo Njau "had set his laws above the Bible",[60] and "that he had made laws that had nothing to do with religion",[61] and that therefore "he quarrelled with the congregation".[62] The most outspoken opposition came from Zakayo Olotu who refused flatly to obey and who sent a letter to Gutmann complaining about the matter.[63] No evidence is available that Gutmann answered by the way of a letter, but that the letter was written shows that many still regarded him to be the pastor in charge and that is how he regarded himself.

Opposition was considerable, therefore very soon disciplinary action had to be taken. First of all exercise books were distributed to all *mitaa* and everyone had to sign that they would not agree to circumcision.[64] Many refused

---

[52] Interview Nahori Malisa 25.5.1971.
[53] Interview Imanuel Mkony 26.7.1971.
[54] Interview Simeon Macha 23.5.1971.
[55] Interview Nahori Malisa 25.5.1971.
[56] Interview Daniel Lyatoo 1970.
[57] Interview Imanuel Mkony 26.7.1971, Paul Fleisch, *Hundert Jahre lutherischer Mission*, p. 417.
[58] Interview Simeon Macha 23.5.1971.
[59] Interview Simeon Macha 23.5.1971.
[60] Interview Daniel Lyatoo 1970.
[61] Interview Petro Moshi 23.5.1971.
[62] Interview Petro Moshi 23.5.1971.
[63] Interview Simeon Macha 23.5.1971.
[64] Interview Nahori Malisa 23.5.1971.

to sign saying: "I have no children of that age, let them (or I shall) decide later on." Those were the lucky ones. Others, who did have children of that age, signed and then circumcised them secretly, telling the people who asked that they were sick.[65] For example a child of Zakayo Olotu was circumcised at night in this way.[66] Others refused to be circumcised at that time but agreed to be circumcised later on.[67] Those offenders who were caught were to be brought before the elders' meeting.[68] They were not dismissed from the church (*kutengwa*), but set apart (*kuwekwa pembeni*, Kichagga: *awiko rihiseni*).[69]

Gutmann returned in April 1926, on the 18.4 the first man came to him to ask for readmission into the church, the second on 24.4, the third on 4.5 etc. On the 5.5.1926 was the first church elders' meeting; the main item on the agenda was the circumcision controversy, and this again on 19.5.26. Gutmann found out the following: Discontent had been widespread also in other congregations, and on the 5.9.1925 the matter had been discussed at Machame: Filipo Njau had attended the meeting and two others. There it had been decided that circumcision was not a reason to put anyone under church discipline. Therefore all punishments should be repealed. Those who went did not inform the elders, Filipo Njau kept quiet and an elder, when later asked why he did not say anything, said that he had not understood the negotiations as they were conducted in Swahili.[70] And when a letter for the elders arrived informing them about the decision of 7.9.1925, Filipo Njau pinched it. And when Hult had ordered him to take the matter before the elders again, he gave the impression that the elders had refused to follow the decisions of 5.9.1925. But in fact they had not even heard of them. Interesting is Gutmann's comment: "What made him so daring to such fraud was the knowledge, that the missionary had access to the congregation only through them".[71] At the first elders' meeting after Gutmann's return he was given authority to reaccept all who had been expelled due to circumcision. This decision was greeted with great relief. After about a year Filipo Njau was called to Marangu to be a teacher at the seminary, a surrounding much more congenial to him.[72]

---

[65] Interview Nahori Malisa 23.5.1971, Interview Ndesanjo Kitange. Immanuel Mkony had no child.
[66] Interview Nahori Malisa 23.5.1971. People knew, but nobody accused him.
[67] Interview Imanuel Mkony 26.5.1971.
[68] Interview Nahori Malisa 23.5.1971.
[69] Interview Nahori Malisa 23.5.1971.
[70] Minutes elders 19.5.1926.
[71] Minutes elders 19.5.1926.
[72] Many years later, Gutmann translated Filipo Njau's autobiography from Chagga into German: Filipo Njau, *Aus meinem Leben* (ed. Martin Küchler), Erlangen: Verlag der Evang.-Luth. Mission, 1960, 56 pp.

This controversy was of great significance for the church. So this seems the place for some observations. That such a far-reaching decision as the abolition of circumcision could be passed unanimously shows that those elders who were supposed to be the representatives of the congregation were not able to present the view of the large majority of the congregation against a vocal minority. This shows that the lay leaders were not efficient enough in dealing with larger issues. Here the lack of knowledge of Swahili becomes striking. The elders had access to the proceeding of the whole church only through the two caretakers. This controversy also shows that it was a disadvantage for the congregation to have a missionary who had no clear grasp of the situation, not that his absence would have avoided the crisis, but his backing of Njau's policy made the situation more difficult. The controversy can also be seen as a result of the refusal of the Leipzig Mission to train Africans for ordination. Had Filipo Njau and Yohane Kimambo and others been trained early as pastors in a thorough course of Lutheran theology, there would have been no need for such a controversy. All these three points were not realized at that time and so steps were taken to remedy the situation. Besides this, here again the chance was missed to integrate circumcision somehow into the life of the church, as it was lost when the matter had come up for discussion for the first time in 1910.

The controversy had far reaching effects: Under Filipo Njau and Yohane Kimambo the congregation had again come closer to modern European civilization, where Chagga society as a whole was moving to. The circumcision controversy destroyed the alliance forged by Gutmann between the church and traditional Chagga culture. Filipo Njau had led the congregation into more modern directions, but here he had gone too far and the reaction was the harder. The old alliance was restored, the grip of traditional Chagga values over the congregation was fastened.

The end of the controversy coincided with the return of Gutmann, technically it was him who ended it. But as a matter of fact it had already been ended by the African leaders themselves, but Filipo Njau had delayed implementing the decision, which then was done by Gutmann. Thus the vast majority of the congregation was happy to be under Gutmann's leadership again.

7. Confirmation and Shield Comradeship

Because Leipzig Mission considered that circumcision was not a religious rite but an *adiaphoron*, Gutmann could not possibly Christianize it or relate it directly to the church's transition rite of confirmation. Circumcision continued in full strength without official relationship to the church; but it had lost its communal character and had become largely a family affair.

Already in the 1910s Gutmann had tried to integrate as much as possible of the teaching connected with circumcision into the teaching of the confirmation candidates and into school teaching, because he had been impressed very early in his career by the valuable teaching the boys received during their seclusion.[73] When he was restricted in his movements after the British occupation of Old Moshi, he used the time to collect all the initiation teachings as the last teaching elders related them, a work which he completed between 1926 and 1929.[74]

Once the circumcision controversy was over, Gutmann tried to transfer the social aspects of circumcision to confirmation, e.g. the organization of the youths into an age group composed of small comradeships. In the traditional Chagga rite, after the circumcision had taken place, the boys lay down two by two and their initiation teachers drew an oval circle around each group of two boys thus binding them together for life in the giving of mutual assistance in all matters.[75]

In 1925 in Masama[76] and the next year in Moshi, he began to use this traditional institution to organize his confirmation classes in groups of two, 'shield comradeships' as they were called according to Chagga tradition.[77] Gutmann's understanding of instruction for confirmation was not only to teach Christian knowledge, but also to get the children used to mutual care within their group[78] and to introduce them to full participation in the life of the congregation.[79] Therefore the two periods of instruction a week were supplemented by one period of service, and so on Saturday the children, shield comradeship by shield comradeship, had to go out to help those mem-

---

[73] Bruno Gutmann, "Eine Jugendlehre bei den Wadschagga", *Evangelisches Missionsblatt*, 1911, pp. 14-21.
[74] The main informants were Malan Malisa, Kyencha Mshiwu and Mlasany Njau from Moshi chiefdom and Ndelishiyo Mboro, Machame (Winter, BLit, p. 102). In the final stages (1926-1929) only Mlasany Njau remained who came every morning very early and dictated one instruction each day over a period of four years. He transmitted these teachings with the express wish that Gutmann should ensure that they were not lost (Bruno Gutmann, *Die Stammeslehren der Dschagga*, 3 vols, München: 1932-1938, I, p. 2).
[75] Bruno Gutmann, *Freies Menschentum aus ewigen Bindungen*, Kassel, 1928, p. 48.
[76] *Evangelisches Missionsblatt*, 1926, pp. 167f.
[77] See Gutmann's articles: "Der Kampf um die Schilde" (*Freies Menschentum aus ewigen Bindungen*, pp. 47-56, (1928), "Der Schildgriff" (*Zurück auf die Gottesstraße*, pp. 22-31 (1934) and "Patenschaft und Konfirmation" (*Zurück auf die Gottesstraße*, pp. 54-56). For Masama see *Evangelisches Missionsblatt*, 1926.
[78] Bruno Gutmann, *Zurück auf die Gottesstraße*, Leipzig, nd. (1938), p. 62.
[79] Ibid., p. 61f. this echoes the Romantic concept that education must be closely related to the community it is to serve, which is also strongly emphasized in the Phelps Stokes Reports.

bers of the congregation who were in need. Gutmann soon realized that for this, the shield comradeships of two were too small, and thus, deviating from the traditional pattern, comradeships of four and six were formed.

The idea of shield comradeship was well received as long as it could be understood in the traditional way: a comradeship for mutual help composed of equals. But when Gutmann instructed them to serve others to whom they were neither related nor obliged, he met with considerable resistance,[80] the strongest coming from those most educated.[81] At first this process of formation of shield comradeships took place during instruction for confirmation, but later Gutmann applied this to school classes in order to keep discipline there and to counterbalance the competitive spirit of the school.[82] In order to solve the problem of what to do with those who were not wanted by anyone in forming a shield comradeship or who were too weak to be equal partners in one, Gutmann arranged that they be put under the patronage of a whole shield comradeship, and though this also met considerable opposition, children soon began to be confirmed in groups of three, five or seven.[83] Gutmann and the elders felt that girls were often not strong enough to help each other, so it was suggested that they should choose one or two older women who were to guide them and to whom in turn they were to give assistance in house and field. Gutmann organized the baptismal classes in a similar way to confirmation classes.[84]

Of the two traditional elements of unity, the small comradeship and the age group as a whole, Gutmann almost exclusively stressed the smaller unit, as for him the age group, "forged in the heat of a transition period", was always in danger of becoming egoistic and antisocial.[85]

When Gutmann introduced these comradeships, the old men were happy, as they were still members of traditional comradeships or saw a chance of reviving

---

[80] Bruno Gutmann, *Freies Menschentum aus ewigen Bindungen*, p. 53.
[81] Bruno Gutmann, *Freies Menschentum aus ewigen Bindungen*, pp. 53-54. Was it that they were more individualized, or were they more able to express feelings common to all?
[82] Attempt and concept described in: *Evangelisches Missionsblatt*, 1927, pp. 31-36 ("Der Kampf um die Schulzucht"), read esp. p. 100. That it was practiced is evident: Gutmann, *Zurück auf die Gottesstraße*, p. 25.
[83] Bruno Gutmann, *Freies Menschentum aus ewigen Bindungen*, p. 50, see also *Zurück auf die Gottesstraße*, pp. 38-21.
[84] Bruno Gutmann, *Zurück auf die Gottesstraße*, pp. 26-28.
[85] Bruno Gutmann, *Christusleib und Nächstenschaft*, Feuchtwangen, 1931, pp. 37f. This view was shared by Johannes Raum (*International Review of Missions*, 1927, p. 589), but not by his neighbour Fritze. For Gutmann the age group was the least important of primal ties and the last he paid attention to (Winter, BLit, p. 296f).

the institution of the age group.⁸⁶ Among younger people the institution found support as well, and even today at Kidia no one is baptized or confirmed alone as an individual. How far the institution retained its Christian content is open for debate, as can be seen from two answers, which were given to the question: What does the shield comradeship mean to you? One interviewee replied: "I pray for each of my shield comrades every day and we help each other."⁸⁷ Another interviewee answered: "When we have our baptismal anniversary, I prepare beer and we visit each other."⁸⁸

Gutmann's combination of confirmation and traditional initiation, incomplete though it was, has proved to be successful. The reason seems to be that it fulfilled the purpose the original rites were designed to fulfill, namely to mark the close of boyhood and the beginning of adulthood, and to give the children the teaching deemed to be necessary. This case shows again that for the acceptance of a certain rite, the manner in which African and European elements were mixed was not decisive, rather the important factor was whether it fulfilled the intended function.

Gutmann's attitude to initiation also illustrates well his conservative approach. Gutmann saw no need for circumcision,⁸⁹ but he made no attempts to suppress it as long as the Chagga themselves were not interested in doing so. He expected that at some later date the Chagga might of their own accord give it up. This change did not take place during his lifetime, but it seems that 40 years after he left Moshi, it did start.⁹⁰

---

⁸⁶ Bruno Gutmann, *Zurück auf die Gottesstraße*, pp. 29-31. Nobody seems to have remembered that in traditional life there was a new age group only after several years, and now each year.
⁸⁷ Interview Kristosia Materu 24.5.1971.
⁸⁸ Interview N.N., Mahoma 28.5.1971.
⁸⁹ He strongly defended the few uncircumcised members of his congregation against unkind comments.
⁹⁰ Since about 1972 a growing number of parents at Old Moshi refuse to have their daughters circumcised (communication Daniel Lyatoo, 1972).

Moshi Congregation and its Conservative Missionary Pastor 1926-1938

The congregation had its pastor back, and well that this happened. Almost everyone was happy how Gutmann solved the intricate circumcision controversy.[1] There was some little demand that Chagga should be ordained as pastors, but not that one of them should replace Gutmann in the near future. Gutmann was secure in his position, and had developed a distinct missionary approach of his own. This approach he had developed largely in Old Moshi, and when he returned in 1926, he was keen to develop his cultural approach to missionary work. Though the congregation would not agree to each of his ideas, he knew that the congregation was in principle willing to go along with him. Limited opposition came from some of the well-trained teachers and other leaders of the progressive segment of Old Moshi society. But even with that segment of society Gutmann managed to keep on good personal terms.

1. Progressives and Conservatives

Susan Rogers in her thesis on the political history of Kilimanjaro[2] uses the dichotomy between the progressive segment of society and the traditional élite represented by the chiefs and their supporters as the main organizing theme for the inter-war period. As there are many parallels between the political developments on Kilimanjaro and the development in Old Moshi congregation, and as Gutmann's views coincided in many aspects with those of the exponents of Indirect Rule her perspective is useful as a background to mine of what happened at Old Moshi in the same period.

In the introduction it was asked if the missionary cultural conservatism and the conservatism of Indirect Rule were the same. It will be seen that Gutmann had many views in common with the colonial administrators on Kilimanjaro, but also that there were important differences in his views and in his actions.

---

[1] Though he seemingly supported the practice of circumcision he made sure that the few members who had opted against circumcision, were neither ridiculed nor molested.

[2] Suzan Geiger Rogers, The Search for Political Focus on Kilimanjaro: A History of Chagga politics, 1916-1952, with special reference to the Cooperative Movement and Indirect Rule, PhD, Dar es Salaam, 1972.

Was missionary cultural conservatism and the conservatism of Indirect Rule the same? Gutmann had many views in common with the colonial administrators on Kilimanjaro, but also there were important differences in his views and in his actions.

Rogers claims that the growing of coffee opened up for the Chagga "the possibility of alternatives, previously not available to them and that this was the critical element in the modernizing process on Kilimanjaro", but that those officials who fostered the growing of coffee did not foresee that it would also provide the major political ferment setting "a rising counter élite backed by an embryonic peasantry" against the traditional authorities backed by the colonial administration.[3]

Rogers sees the Kilimanjaro Native Planters' Association (KNPA) as an attempt of the progressives not only to organize coffee marketing more effectively, but also to achieve a greater participation in the affairs of their society. By dismantling the KNPA and replacing it by the KNCU[4], which was de facto the economic arm of the administrative machinery, they were taught

> that there was to be no such thing as permissible, legitimate unofficial political expression, much less organization outside the Native Authority System which effectively excluded them and whose representatives (chiefs and supporters) were felt to be at best ineffective in dealing with the protection of Chagga interests vis-à-vis the government and at worst, openly hostile to change for fear of losing their own positions.[5]

Though the concept of Indirect Rule as described by Cameron[6] included the idea that gradually the pattern of the chiefs' rule had to be changed to make it less authoritarian and more representative, nothing in fact changed during the first 20 years of Indirect Rule on Kilimanjaro.[7] The colonial authorities continually reminded the Chagga progressives that the chiefs were their only "lawful and natural mentors"[8] and that there was no room for any divergent aspirations. Thus the 1930s ended in frustration for the progressives. The

---

[3] Suzan Geiger Rogers, The Search for Political Focus on Kilimanjaro, p. 234.
[4] Kilimanjaro Native Cooperative Union.
[5] Suzan Geiger Rogers, The Search for Political Focus on Kilimanjaro, p. 512.
[6] Donald Cameron, "Native Administration in Nigeria and Tanganyika", Extra Supplement of the *Journal of the Royal African Society*, vol. 26, 1937.
[7] Old Moshi congregation had 2135 members in 1925 (Staude - Fiedler 10.4.1975). 1926-1930 there were 1107 adult baptisms (Baptism registers, Kidia).
[8] Bruno Gutmann described his concept of dealing with the problems of accelerated social change and growing church membership in a talk to the 1927 missionary conference: "Church discipline in a new era" (minutes missionary conference 30.8.1927).

chiefs' position became increasingly dependent on the exclusive support of the colonial authorities. Finally the chiefs were swept away as being redundant not long after independence, and political power in Tanzania passed completely into the hands of the progressives.

This chapter deals with Gutmann's second period at Old Moshi. Whereas Gutmann had been able to develop his conservative approach in the comparative quietness of the 1910s, now he had to prove, under the pressure of accelerating social change, what it was worth.

In such a situation of progressive aspirations and some colonial repression Gutmann had to prove his cultural missionary approach as viable. His congregation contained members who were part of the progressive élite, but had a large more conservative majority.

2. The Further Development of Gutmann's Cultural Approach

When Gutmann came back to Tanzania he realized that much more change had taken place than he had expected. The membership of the congregation had grown considerably, the impact of European civilization had made itself felt much more strongly and the time of paternalistic missionary rule was gone. Gutmann was convinced that the church had to take up the challenge of change, and he was convinced that his concept of the organic congregation showed the way to go, and that traditional Chagga culture contained many remedies for the ills of society.

Before the war Gutmann had tried primarily to use the primal tie of the clan for strengthening the church, and he had taken account of the growth of the congregation by election of location elders and agricultural supervisors and by establishing the location councils.

On his return to Tanzania in 1925 he had organized the baptismal and confirmation classes into shield comradeships. In later years he again used the same method in schools to keep discipline and to avoid estrangement of the children from their social context.[9]

A further major step in the development of his concept of the organic congregation was the institution of Christian neighbourhoods. Already before 1920 rapidly growing numbers of church members had previously led Gutmann to decentralize and to lay increasing emphasis on the locations, for example by holding the preparation for the celebration of Holy Communion there.

---

[9] See "Schule und Volk", Bruno Gutmann, *Unter dem Trutzbaum: Eine Einkehr in Moshi am Kilimanjaro*, Leipzig, nd. [1938], pp. 99-106.

But soon locations proved too large. In 1928 when the distribution of part of the harvest festival offerings to the needy was discussed, one elder said that assistance once a year was not enough, and that therefore they had subdivided their location into neighbourhoods.[10] Each neighbourhood had elected two elders to organize mutual assistance, to care for the spiritual well being of all church members there and to keep contact with the elders of the location and with the pastor.[11] This arrangement impressed the other elders and early in 1929 all locations were subdivided into neighbourhoods. In 1931 the preparation for Holy Communion was transferred from the location to the neighbourhoods where the people really knew each other.[12] To Gutmann this innovation was not merely a matter of more efficient church organization but an implementation of his policy to relate the church to the primal ties, and thereby also to Chagga social structure in which the neighbourhoods played a significant role. As the establishment of Christian neighbourhoods was congenial to the existing social order, the neighbourhoods became an effective tool for the management of the congregation.[13]

Although Gutmann had experienced little response before the war to his attempts to revitalize the clan structure, he tried again. This time he wanted to use the moral force of the clan elders to support Christian morality. He instituted an advisory board of clan heads whose purpose was to support and advise the elders on matters related to morality and Chagga culture. This council met twice a year, together with the elders of the congregation. But this advisory council never fulfilled Gutmann's expectations, because the clan heads were losing influence rapidly.[14]

In order to make the sacrament of (infant) baptism meaningful to the children as they grew up, Gutmann stressed very much the office of sponsorship. This office had roots in the European Christian tradition as well as in traditional African society. It was an accepted custom in Germany, but sponsors (*wangari*) were also a common feature in the rites and institutions of tradi-

---

[10] Each neighbourhood comprised those who got their water for irrigation from the same furrow.
[11] Bruno Gutmann, "Die Gemeinde", *Das Gottesjahr*, 1939, p. 56 gives no date. But internal evidence and comparison with the elders' minutes book shows that it was the session of 3.10.1928. See also minutes elders 17.10.1928.
[12] Minutes neighbourhood leaders 25.8.1931. In 1934 Moshi-Mbokomu congregation had 13 locations divided into 38 neighbourhoods, each neighbourhood comprising an average of 130 Christians (information kindly supplied by Winter - Fiedler 17.12.1971). See also Gutmann, *Unter dem Trutzbaum*, p. 118.
[13] After his return to Germany he repeatedly strongly recommended that the churches in Germany adopt the principle of neighbourhoods following the example given by the Chagga.
[14] This idea made some missionaries accuse Gutmann of wanting to supplant the church by the natural social organization and of paying more attention to things social than to things spiritual (Paul Fleisch, *Hundert Jahre lutherischer Mission*, pp. 441-419).

tional Chagga society. Gutmann held regular meetings with the sponsors who had to accompany their godchildren to church at their baptism anniversary and he instituted the controversial rule that sponsors who had died or were excommunicated had to be replaced by substitute sponsors. This replacement was resented widely, but if sponsorship was to be more than Christian folklore, it was only logical.

The sponsors very often were close relatives who even in traditional life would have had responsibility for the child concerned, and they were to guide their godchildren until they received Holy Communion for the first time. Then the child would be integrated into the new relationships based on the primal tie of the age group.

After confirmation the young people formed an age group (*rika*) under a *rika* leader in each location who was assisted by a dancing ground supervisor chosen from among the elders.

With the introduction of the new institutions described above, Gutmann had, so to say, put the final touches on the organization of his congregation. He did not consider the congregation to be a mass of individuals all centred on the pastor but rather an organic body, consisting of different estates and groups, all interacting with each other and every group caring for its members. With these arrangements Gutmann had managed to relate every Christian to several others, and everyone could find and give spiritual and practical assistance whenever needed. Gutmann as pastor of such a large congregation did not feel his task to be mainly to care for the individual, but to train and lead these organic groupings to fulfill their duties. This he mainly implemented by holding regular meetings not only with the elders but with agricultural supervisors, neighbourhood leaders, dancing ground supervisors, age group leaders, and sponsors, and whenever the need arose, he met with the whole congregation of a given location or with its teacher(s) and school elders. Through all the different institutions the church was organically related to Chagga social order. This means that the church had become a real folk-church.

In thus organizing the church on lines relevant to traditional Chagga society Gutmann consciously avoided employing certain methods of church organization, which he had known from Germany. As a boy he had himself been a member of the YMCA, and had received much spiritual guidance through it,[15] yet he did not start a YMCA branch at Old Moshi. Instead he

---

[15] Bruno Gutmann writes that through the YMCA he heard the call to become a missionary (Ernst Jaeschke, "Ein Leben für Afrikaner" in Bruno Gutmann, "*Afrikaner – Europäer in nächstenschaftlicher Entsprechung*, p. 14).

devised the *rika* meetings and the Sunday afternoon dances. The dances were surely a good Chagga custom, but little adaptable to changing circumstances, whereas a YMCA branch could have arranged the dances, and been more adaptable to change. But Gutmann did not favour voluntary associations, neither in church nor, as will be shown later, in politics.

In organizing his congregation, Gutmann had based many of his institutions on similar institutions in traditional society, but society was changing fast. Gutmann did not deny the right to change, but it must be asked if these traditional institutions were able to accommodate change. The same question has been asked of the institutions of Indirect Rule, and a largely negative answer must be given.[16] This is not true to the same extent for Old Moshi. Some of the institutions that Gutmann created were more likely to continue even after considerable changes in society because they could be adapted to new circumstances. Examples of this were the neighbourhoods and the shield comradeships, but others like the clan elders' advisory council and the Sunday afternoon dances became anachronistic. Gutmann had managed to organize a congregation of more than 4000 members in a remarkable way,[17] but he had not given it a structure, which could easily adapt to the many changes that Chagga society was to undergo.

---

[16] Kenneth Robinson, *The Dilemmas of Trusteeship*, London: OUP, 1965, p. 87.
[17] Ernst Jaeschke, who became Gutmann's successor in 1938, stated that without this organization he would never have been able to lead this congregation of more than 5000 members properly (Ernst Jaeschke, "Introduction" to Bruno Gutmann, *Afrikaner – Europäer in nächstenschaftlicher Entsprechung*, p. 25).

Gutmann's Concept of African Leadership

Gutmann's cultural conservatism finds a strong expression in his concept of African leadership. How this concept diverged from what one might call the progressive view of leadership, can best be exemplified by juxtaposing Filipo Njau and Imanuel Mkony, Gutmann's assistants during his first and second period at Old Moshi respectively.

1. Immanuel Mkony Replaces Filipo Njau

When Gutmann first came to Old Moshi, Imanuel Mkony had already been a teacher for about six years and he was quite competent. He had wanted to go to the seminary, but Gutmann had told him to be content with what he had.[1] Over all the years Imanuel Mkony had been active in church work[2] and when Filipo Njau left to teach at Marangu Seminary, Mkony seemed to be the obvious choice to fill his place.

But still this change was very significant. Mkony and Njau were different characters, personifying different eras and different aspirations. Their background was similar, both came from the boarding school at Kidia, but when Imanuel Mkony was refused permission to go to Marangu Seminary and when Filipo Njau went, they developed differently. Filipo Njau became who he was mainly by being trained, while Imanuel Mkony developed more by growing with his job and proving his worth in it. Mkony was more strongly related to his local area, whereas Filipo Njau had wide contacts with his fellow teachers.

Imanuel Mkony definitely fitted much better into Gutmann's concept of African leadership, which he felt was best left to develop within the congregation to avoid alienation of the leaders from the 'ordinary' Christians. For Gutmann this view never excluded training at a seminary or theological school though some of Gutmann's adherents among the younger missionaries felt this to be so.

---

[1] Interview Imanuel Mkony 26.5.1971.
[2] He also did the pioneer missionary work in malaria infested Kahe (Interview Immanuel Mkony 26.5.1971 and Mkony - Gutmann 21.6.1924).

2. Ordination of African Pastors

Marcia Wright states that Gutmann objected on principle to the ordination of African pastors, but if he ever had such objections, he always fully cooperated with the plans of ordaining Africans.[3]

As a whole, the Lutherans and Moravians in Tanzania were very slow in ordaining African pastors.[4] But with growing membership and education, even the Lutherans could not keep their eyes shut any longer. At the 1927 missionary conference the need to train the first 'ordained assistants' was recognized.[5] Against this, Leipzig, which had pressed for speedy training of pastors before, stressed that no missionaries' assistants should be trained but independent pastors.[6] In 1930 the first General Church Conference greeted with enthusiasm the decision to ordain African pastors[7] and the first ordination course (January 1933 - April 1934) was started under Raum in Machame,[8] with 14 candidates, twelve of them having been caretakers before.[9]

From Old Moshi congregation Imanuel Mkony was the first to be chosen. Some teachers complained that he did not know English and suggested sending Filipo Njau instead who at that` time was teacher at Marangu Seminary.[10] Gutmann answered that for the pastors' training English was not necessary, but the discussion showed again the divergence between Gutmann and the teachers. Isaki Shayo, the candidate for Mbokomu, could not find the necessary support of Mbokomu congregation;[11] instead of him Ndesanjo Kitange was chosen, a native of Mowo, a seminary-trained teacher, but not a caretaker.[12]

The ordination course was held in Swahili and the students had to write down a lot (both pastors still have and use the notes they made at Machame).

---

[3] Marcia Wright, *German Missions in Tanganyika 1891-1941: Lutherans and Moravians in the Southern Highlands*, Oxford: Clarendon, 1971, p. 178. She refers to Paul Fleisch, *Hundert Jahre lutherischer Mission*, pp. 418f, p. 444, which has no reference to Gutmann's objections. Joseph Merinyo claims credit for having convinced Gutmann of the need to ordain Africans. But the missionary conference of 1931 had already decided on steps to implement the insight of the 1927 conference.
[4] Only Bethel ordained Africans when the missionaries had to leave in 1920, and the Berlin missionary Martin Priebusch had ordained Martin Ganisya.
[5] Minutes missionary conference 1927, decision 35; see also Paul Fleisch, *Hundert Jahre lutherischer Mission*, p. 411.
[6] Paul Fleisch, *Hundert Jahre lutherischer Mission*, p. 440.
[7] Paul Fleisch, *Hundert Jahre lutherischer Mission*, p. 443.
[8] For his concept for the training and the work of the pastors see, "Stellung unserer eingeborenen Hirten im Ganzen unserer Arbeit. Thesen J. Raum" (minutes missionary conference 1933).
[9] Paul Fleisch, *Hundert Jahre lutherischer Mission*, p. 444. He mistakenly counts 13.
[10] Minutes elders 11.10.1932.
[11] Minutes elders 11.2.1932.
[12] Interview Ndesanjo Kitange 27.5.1971. Paul Fleisch was not aware of this change (p. 444).

There were 24 lessons a week, including church history, mission history with a special emphasis on Africa, and Islam. For that time the course was quite thorough with a large component of practical theology.[13] After ordination Imanuel Mkony was posted to Mbokomu and he also supervised the missionary work at Okuma and Uru.[14] Kitange lived at Kidia but did his work mainly in what is today Shia congregation and in the outpost of Msaranga. He also supervised the missionary work at Kahe.[15]

With this arrangement Gutmann had posted both pastors to important sections of the congregation (east and west) and thus given them quite independent positions whereas in most other congregations the pastors stayed with the missionary and were much more dependent.[16] With the ordination of African pastors the missionaries had created the first position of higher leadership in the church open to Africans, which was not based on ascriptive role but on achieved role. It is true that the newly ordained pastors were still under missionary control, even at Old Moshi, but they were given responsibility at a time when the colonial authorities on Kilimanjaro strongly refused to let the progressives have any role of leadership.

Though the missionaries and the progressives both had supported the training of African pastors,[17] their office still reflected the cultural conservatism not only of Gutmann but also of his mission as a whole, because it was differently structured from that of their European colleagues. In his talk during the 1930 missionary conference George Fritze, pastor of neighbouring Mamba congregation, began by stating that the pastors should remain Africans in their thinking and in their feeling.[18] No African would have doubted that, but the fact that it was stated in such a prominent place in his talk leaves room for the suspicion that this statement had some oppressive overtones.

---

[13] Paul Fleisch, *Hundert Jahre lutherischer Mission*, p. 44, see also J. Raum, "Heranbildung eingeborener Pastoren für die Gemeinden der Evg.-Luth. Mission zu Leipzig in Ostafrika", *Neue Allgemeine Missionszeitschrift*, 1933, pp. 22-34.
[14] Minutes elders 2.7.1935, see also Interview Imanuel Mkony 26.5.1971.
[15] Interview Ndesanjo Kitange 27.5.1971.
[16] Observed with acclaim by inspector Küchler (visitation report Küchler 1937). In order to guide the pastors in their work he produced a detailed guide for pastors, a document that would be of considerable value even for today's pastoral work: "Einweisung in den Hirtendienst an einer christlichen Gemeinde", published only in German translation, first in *Dorfkirche*, 1941, pp. 58ff, then after the war in *Lutherische Blätter*, 1960, no. 65, pp. 40-53. Most easily accessible in Gutmann, *Afrikaner - Europäer*, pp. 150-167. Peter Beyerhaus, *Die Selbständigkeit der jungen Kirchen*, Wuppertal, 1956, does not seem to have taken notice that in Gutmann's congregation there were two African pastors.
[17] The support of the progressives was obviously so strong that it is often depicted that the missionaries gave in to their demands.
[18] "The training of our ordained assistants". Minutes missionary conference 1930.

59

Another important fact is that for this ordination course only men could be chosen who had proven their worth in the service of their congregation, and that, of necessity, meant older men.[19] This has to be compared to the fact that no missionary had undergone such a selection process, all having received their training as quite young men. But African pastors, even more than African teachers, were not to become a professional class, but "should remain deeply rooted in their surroundings".[20] This was also accentuated by the policy that an African pastor should normally serve the congregation from which he came, as this would provide the "necessary prerequisites for fruitful service".[21] These three points made sure that the roles of the African pastors and their missionary colleagues remained different, with the missionaries claiming that the position of the African pastors would thus be more fitting to African culture.[22]

3. Gutmann and the Elders

It is not surprising that Gutmann and the progressives often clashed. But it is astonishing that on many issues the elders, though they were Gutmann's natural allies, could not agree with him. Gutmann's relationship to the elders will be traced in some detail in three major issues: The increasing consumption of beer, the increasing number of unblessed marriages and the conflict between the elders and the youths over the Sunday afternoon dances. It will be seen that the elders' conservatism was different from Gutmann's. His aim was to use as many elements as possible from traditional culture to solve the problems of the present, whereas the elders' main aim was to preserve the status quo. They had to defend their position against any encroachment and tended to see the use of certain traditional elements not as conservatism but as innovation.[23] The elders feared any innovation; regardless of the grounds it was suggested on, which might endanger their dominating role. In this

---

[19] Nearly all were older than 40 (*Evangelisches Missionsblatt*, 1931, p. 18).
[20] Minutes missionary conference 1927: "The teachers must be rooted in the soil and not become a professional class."
[21] Johannes Raum: "Die Stellung unserer eingeborenen Hirten im Ganzen unserer Arbeit" (minutes missionary conference 1930). A few years later Ihmels, the director of the Leipzig Mission, came to doubt very much this assumption. He wrote: "I am strongly convinced that in this concept there is one of the greatest dangers of our African mission" (Ihmels - Müller 30.6.1937).
[22] The difference is explicitly stated in J. Raum, "Die Hirtenschule in Madschame", *Lutherisches Missionsjahrbuch*, 1934, pp. 142-149 (see p. 145).
[23] Cf. J.B. Webster, *The African Churches among the Yoruba 1888-1922*, Oxford: Clarendon, 1964 p. 120.

their attitude was paralleled by that of the traditional élite under Indirect Rule.

Lema, in his analysis of missionaries' attitudes to Chagga culture, states that the missionaries "never bothered to find out the true meaning of *mbeke* (beer) drinking in Kilimanjaro".[24] If this was so, Gutmann surely was an exception. He knew well that "*mbeke* beer was never bought and sold" and that it was usually brewed for specific purposes such as family, clan, or community festivals, bride wealth, circumcision, and initiation ceremonies.[25] Gutmann also knew very well which parts of the bride wealth had to be given in beer, which parts had to be accompanied by gifts of beer and who was supposed to drink this beer. He also knew that in traditional Chagga social order the drinking of beer was controlled by the headmen and elders who were especially careful to keep children away.

He was well aware of all this, and although he himself did not drink any beer, he never said a word against its drinking if confined within the traditional order of things. But he observed that things had changed. With the increasing freedom of the individual in Chagga society and expansion of the money economy, beer became more readily available; it was now a purchasable commodity. Supervision of the drinking of beer by the elders became less strict, and even girls began to prepare beer on their own and to invite their fiancés. Also the amount of beer required for the different exchanges of bride wealth had grown considerably.[26]

To combat excessive drinking, Gutmann appealed to the old order of things.[27] He charged the elders to play the role of controllers, as would have been their duty in traditional society. But they did not take up this customary role. Then he made the congregation pass a law that there should be no beer at Christmas. But this law was kept in three locations only, and in the other locations the elders were among those most prominent in providing beer.[28] Had they not provided beer, this would have endangered their social status.

---

[24] Anza Amen Lema, The Impact of the Leipzig Lutheran Mission on the People of Kilimanjaro, PhD, University of Dar es Salaam, 1973, p. 587.
[25] Ibid.
[26] For the Lutherans consumption of beer was an *adiaphoron*. Even a missionary who did not like beer could not forbid its drinking, as it was done in a number of Presbyterian missions like Livingstonia and Nkhoma in Malawi. Entry elders 7.11.1926 shows that Gutmann was aware of these changes.
[27] He also included into the congregation's hymn and service book a section on what the Bible teaches about the dangers of alcoholic beverages, this being quite a unique feature in a hymnbook: "Madedo hekapana na wukuwu wo wari na wunanzi". ("Words which oppose the love of beer and drunkenness"), *Kitabu kya siri* (1931), pp. 150-152.
[28] Beer being an adiaphoron the missionary could not make a law concerning consumption of beer, but the congregation on its own initiative could do so. Gutmann tried to 'stimulate' this initiative.

To reduce the amount of beer consumed during the *wari wo tila* (playbeer)[29] when the bridegroom for the first time "shows his house to his fiancée", Gutmann made neighbourhood leaders discuss the matter and it was decided to follow again traditional practice: "Only once, only one container, only the nearest relatives, only if the bride is accompanied by an elder sister and the bridegroom by his sponsor (*mngari*).[30] For some time these rules were kept,[31] but here also the appeal to traditional order was not taken up by the elders of the congregation. Any reduction in the provision of beer would have endangered the leading position of the elders; as such a leading position in society was not imaginable without the generous entertainment of guests.

With a similar approach, namely the appeal to the old order, Gutmann tried to solve another thorny pastoral problem of those years. This problem was the rapidly growing number of young couples who were marrying without the blessing of the church and even without fulfilling all the many necessary traditional requirements.

The issue had arisen for general discussion in the elders' meeting for the first time when Fritze was in charge of Old Moshi during Gutmann's 1930/31 leave. Unblessed marriages were seen as "opposed to all divine and human order", and a prolonged period of church discipline was suggested.[32] After his return Gutmann called a meeting of elders, age group leaders and dancing ground supervisors to discuss the problem. It was decided to attempt to reduce the costs of a wedding and to reduce the amount of beer consumed at the *wari wo tila*. But all this did not lead to a decrease in the number of unblessed marriages.

By 1933 it had been realized that expulsion from full church membership was not being taken seriously,[33] because the offenders were accepted back after some time anyway. It was also realized that to extend the time of expulsion to six years would be unjust to those who agreed to an unblessed marriage under pressure.[34] To help such couples Gutmann suggested creating a legal way for girls to hasten their marriage, based again on traditional precedents. The girl should not go to her future husband, but to her mother-in-law, thus forcing the marriage arrangements to be made more speedily, and after

---

[29] This is the translation Gutmann uses (*Spielbier*). Yakobo L. Lyimo - Fiedler 20.5.1975 gives *pombe ya mazungumzo* (beer of conversation) as it is consumed slowly while the bride's and the bridegroom's people chat.
[30] Minutes neighbourhood leaders 23.6.1932.
[31] Minutes age group leaders 6.9.1932.
[32] Fritze wrote in annual report Moshi 1930: "They come together like cattle".
[33] Bruno Gutmann stated this explicitly in annual report Moshi 1933. By 1933 even Fritze had accepted that such marriages were not fornication but real marriages (annual report Mamba 1933).
[34] Minutes elders 27.6.1933.

finalizing the agreements, there should be a full church ceremony without any shame on the couple.[35]

This suggestion did not meet with much enthusiasm among the elders. Whereas the neighbourhood leaders agreed to Gutmann's proposal, the elders refused.[36] Somehow Gutmann still managed to introduce this rule on the hastening of a marriage and in his annual report for 1933 he noted that this new rule had saved three couples from church discipline.[37] Not much more seems to have resulted from this idea. This is understandable because the only solution could have been to shorten in a drastic way the lengthy and costly process of getting married, but this would have helped further to reduce the already diminishing authority of the older over the younger generation.

Interestingly this case has similarities with the circumcision controversy. Many missionaries before the war had been highly critical of circumcision and had hoped to have it abolished. The caretakers' attitude to circumcision in 1923 reflected the missionaries' position of a couple of years previously. Likewise around 1930 the missionaries had loudly condemned unblessed marriages and the elders had taken the same view. By 1933 Gutmann and even Fritze had second thoughts. They began to accept such marriages as real marriages and were willing to look for some accommodation with the changed practice, but the elders stuck to the missionaries' attitude of three years earlier.

Another problem troubling Gutmann and the elders was the fact that on Sundays after attending church the young people lacked proper entertainment. To solve this problem, Gutmann had introduced the Sunday dances for the youth. These dances were held every Sunday afternoon in every location. The age group leader of the location was responsible for the youths' behaviour and the dancing ground supervisor assisted him. The congregation appointed both.

Very soon after Gutmann went to Germany in 1930 the elders forbade these Sunday afternoon dances because they felt that the youths did not behave properly and that they did not show the required respect to their elders.[38] Gutmann was angry that the elders had forbidden the dances unilaterally. On his return he made the age group leaders, dancing-ground supervi-

---

[35] Minutes neighbourhood leaders 4.7.1933.
[36] Minutes elders 11.7.1933.
[37] Annual report Moshi 1933.
[38] They criticized especially the sharp tongue of the youths. Satirical ditties and mocking songs were a frequent feature of the singing of Chagga youths (Otto Raum, *Chagga Childhood*, London: OUP, 1940, p. 223).

sors and neighbourhood leaders discuss the problem, but even after the youths had accepted quite stringent rules for supervising the Sunday dances, in June 1933 the elders still refused permission to reopen the dances because they felt that with the state of the youth being as it was, it would be impossible to supervise the dances, to which one of the age group leaders replied:

"If there are no dances, misbehaviour will spread more rapidly and supervision will be even more difficult. When there are no dances, the young people leave their parents' compound right after the morning service to visit each other or to roam about uncontrollably."[39]

The youths repeated their request only to be refused permission finally in November 1932.[40] The victory of age over youth was decisive. None of the problems had been solved by this decision; the older generation had simply asserted its authority (or what they perceived it to be). Whereas in traditional society the warrior age group was the dominating age group, in the church the elders had, over the years, become the dominant age group. They had not forbidden the dances because they did not like Chagga culture or because they feared syncretism, they simply felt challenged in their dominant role and they reacted in a typically authoritarian way.

Though the decision of November 1932 was supposed to be final, about two years later Gutmann succeeded, after another prolonged period of negotiations due to the growing pressure of the youths, in reversing the decision, and in January 1935 the dancing grounds were reopened.[41]

Up to the present time all the issues discussed above have not been solved in Kidia congregation: The consumption of beer continued to grow, the cleavage between the generations is considerable and unblessed marriages are accepted as the usual thing.

4. Gutmann and the Educational System

Gutmann has often been depicted as the arch tribalist among the missionaries and as being opposed to any kind of Western influence on Africans. Susan Rogers speaks of the old guard Leipzigers, led by Gutmann, realizing in 1932 that central school education did not have the bad effects on the pupils

---

[39] Minutes age group leaders 12.7.1932.
[40] Minutes neighbourhood leaders 22.11.1932.
[41] Minutes elders 8.1.1935. The negotiations: Minutes age group leaders 8.7.1934, neighbourhood leaders 17.7.1934, neighbourhood and age group leaders 2.10.1934, elders and age group leaders 23.10.1934, elders and neighbourhood leaders 6.11.1934, elders 4.12.1934.

they had expected.[42] Johanna Eggert in her study of the educational effort of the German Protestant Missions in Tanzania[43] goes so far as to state that Gutmann wanted to bar Africans from getting to know any other culture than their own and that he completely rejected European education for Africans.[44]

The Leipzig Mission had always had the best educational system of the German Protestant Missions and before World War I, Old Moshi congregation had for that time a good primary school system. Due to the willingness of the teachers to work for years with no pay, or very little, the school system was still in good shape when Gutmann returned. Between 1925 and 1928 the educational system of Tanzania was restructured according to the new policy of cooperation between government and missions that found its most tangible expression in the grant-in-aid system.[45]

Right from the start Gutmann strongly supported the new programme to improve the Leipzig school system by establishing so-called model schools, which qualified for a government subsidy, and by providing certified teachers. He was aware that an improved school system would be a challenge to his cultural approach, but he was willing to take the risk.[46] In 1928 it was necessary to decide if the mission was to accept government grants and bring its school system to the required standard or not. Superintendent Raum was against it; Eduard Ittameier felt that as a German he could not accept grants, which were designed to "Anglicize the inhabitants of a colony that by right should be German".[47] Only Paul Rother, Head of the Marangu Seminary, and the 'arch-conservative' Gutmann were definitely in favour of taking grants. In the end grants were accepted nevertheless, and in 1928/9 the school system of the mission was being reformed. The November meeting of the elders of Old Moshi congregation had to be attended by supplementary delegates from each location to discuss the reform of the school system. The schools were to be integrated more into the life of the congregation and of society as a whole. To reach this aim for every school about six school elders were

---

[42] Suzan Geiger Rogers, The Search for Political Focus on Kilimanjaro, p. 528 referring to Marcia Wright, German Evangelical Missions in Tanganyika, 1891-1939, with Special Reference to the Southern Highlands, PhD, London University, 1966, p. 347.
[43] Johanna Eggert, *Missionsschule und sozialer Wandel in Ostafrika*, Bielefeld: Bertelsmann, 1970.
[44] Johanna Eggert, *Missionsschule und sozialer Wandel in Ostafrika*, pp. 210 and 212-213.
[45] Roland Oliver, *The Missionary Factor in East Africa*, 1967 edition, pp. 263-281; Johanna Eggert, *Missionsschule und sozialer Wandel in Ostafrika*, pp. 197-220.
[46] Minutes missionary conference 1928, also Gutmann, *Gemeindeaufbau aus dem Evangelium*, p. 129.
[47] Minutes missionary conference 20.8.1928. Fritze, Blumer and Eisenschmidt expressed their solidarity with Raum's and Ittameier's opinion during the same session.

chosen.⁴⁸ Additionally, model schools were to be established in major locations of the congregation.

Soon Old Moshi congregation had four model schools (Kidia, Mbokomu, Tela and Shia).⁴⁹ In spite of the dangers Gutmann saw in the school system, he gave his full support to its expansion. When Fritze replaced Gutmann in 1930 he felt that Gutmann had established far too many schools and that it would be better if he closed some of them.⁵⁰ But after his return Gutmann again did everything he could to expand further, complaining bitterly that in 1930 a healthy development had been interrupted by Fritze.⁵¹ The congregation shared this attitude to the extent that when money became scarce due to the slump in world coffee prices all insisted that no schools should be closed.⁵²

In order to guarantee that the schools were not disrupting Chagga folkhood, Gutmann demanded that the schools, besides caring for the mother tongue, tribal culture and values, should be rooted in the primal ties. This he attempted by basing all school discipline on comradeships, which were assisted by elders from the boys' home areas, who thus provided the link to clan and neighbourhood.⁵³ In very many issues Paul Rother of Marangu was Gutmann's closest ally,⁵⁴ and had the outbreak of the Second World War not prevented his return, Gutmann would have been placed at Marangu as Superintendent of the mission and coordinator of the various schools at Marangu and of the whole educational system.⁵⁵

Another Lutheran missionary had to face the same issue, and though he came to the same conclusion, he did reach it with different arguing. Ernst Johanssen, Bethel missionary first in Usambara and later in Bukoba,⁵⁶ had to face the same problem of advanced education after his return to Tanzania. He had attended the educational conference in Dar es Salaam in 1925,⁵⁷ and he was convinced that full cooperation with the government was necessary

---

⁴⁸ This was one of the basic demands of the Phelps-Stokes-Commission and of cultural conservatism alike. Minutes elders 7.11.1928.
⁴⁹ Annual report Moshi 1930 (written by Fritze).
⁵⁰ Annual report Moshi 1934.
⁵¹ Annual report Moshi 1933.
⁵² Minutes elders 17.11.1931, 8.12.1931.
⁵³ This demand is described in Gutmann, *Christusleib und Nächstenschaft*, pp. 230-233. For how he tried to put this into practice see Gutmann, *Unter dem Trutzbaum*, pp. 99-106. See also Gutmann, *Freies Menschentum aus ewigen Bindungen*, pp. 93-94 and *Zurück auf die Gottesstraße*, pp. 25-26.
⁵⁴ Interview Rudolf Rother 29.4.1973.
⁵⁵ Letter missionary council - Leipzig Board 17.8.1939.
⁵⁶ For his life see: *Führung und Erfahrung im vierzigjährigen Missionsdienst*, 3 vols., Bethel: nd.
⁵⁷ Johanssen published extensive extracts from his diaries of this time in *Führung und Erfahrung im vierzigjährigen Missionsdienst*, III, pp. 99-114.

and possible and that the teaching of English was the clear wish of the African Christians in general.[58] So Lwandai was established as a Central School with English as the medium of instruction. Other Bethel missionaries in Usambara opposed this. Franz Gleiß had protested already in 1925 against any unnecessary emphasis on education.[59] In 1928 the Usambara missionaries under the leadership of Wohlrab decided (while Johanssen was away in Bukoba) against the opinion of Miss Lindner, the head teacher of the school, to replace English by Swahili as the medium of instruction, in order not to estrange the future leaders from their fellow countrymen. But English was to be kept as a subject.[60] Johanssen was furious, the Director of Education replied that the government could not produce for each school a separate set of regulations.[61] Bethel had no clear position, nor had Bodelschwingh, the Director of the Mission in Germany, but soon the problem was solved by the fact that the Department of Education recognized Lwandai as a Central School although only English and Mathematics had English as the medium of instruction, the other subjects being taught in Swahili, with religious instruction in Shambala, the language of Usambara.[62]

Both Gutmann and Johanssen actually supported English as medium of instruction in Central Schools. The difference was in attitude. Gutmann felt it to be a necessity because the government demanded it. Contrary to this Johanssen believed that everyone should develop his capacities to the utmost, and just as a German would do well to learn English, so would an African.[63] Johanssen was combining, both a high regard for African culture, and full appreciation of African modernizing aspirations, whereas Gutmann did not see the intrinsic value of teaching English but was willing to accommodate the Africans' demand for it.[64]

---

[58] *Evangelisches Missionsmagazin*, 1930, p. 58.
[59] Franz Gleiß - Arbeistausschuf der Bethel Mission 21.9.1925.
[60] Karl Wohlrab - Bethel Board 5.4.1928.
[61] Ernst Johanssen – Friedrich von Bodelschwingh 13.9.1928. In 1930 Johanssen published an article defending the African demand for English education which caused a very mixed reaction in German missionary circles (Ernst Johanssen, "Heraus aus der Isolierung", *Neue Allgemeine Missionszeitschrift*, 1930). On the whole issue see also Marcia Wright, *German Missions in Tanganyika*, 198f.
[62] Johanna Eggert, *Missionsschule und sozialer Wandel in Ostafrika*, p. 247.
[63] Ernst Johanssen – Friedrich von Bodelschwingh 13.9.1928.
[64] Johanssen's family had strong relations to England which were not severed because of the war. Gutmann's attitude to English was ambivalent, he tried never to be unfair but was convinced that British and Americans in general were not able or willing to understand other cultures. This makes it possible that sentiments of nationalism play a role in his opposition to English, but if he had these sentiments, he never allowed them to come into the open in his writings.

5. The Fritze - Merinyo Controversy and the Coffee Riots

The previous section has shown that although cultural conservatism and the aspirations of the educated élite were poles apart, full cooperation in educational matters was possible, while somewhat uneasy group- and sometimes personal relationships remained. The controversy over dress between Fritze and Merinyo elucidates further the clash of aspirations between the educated élite and a missionary, but it also shows that not all culturally conservative missionaries were alike because it ended up with the conservative Gutmann defending the progressive Merinyo against the authoritarian Fritze. The coffee riots provide a chance to see missionary cultural conservatism in the larger context of the political awakening of a group, which challenged the established chiefs' authority.

Before the war Chagga Christians had been wearing mostly what the missionaries spoke of as African dress, namely the *kanzu*.[65] When in the 1930s many began to acquire European clothes, many missionaries regarded this as a symbol of destruction of Chagga folkhood.

European dress also symbolized the process of growing social differentiation in Chagga society, a thing many missionaries resented strongly. For the Chagga, especially for the educated and for those earning cash, European dress was the symbol of social advancement and of the beginning of attempts to throw off European domination. This explains why the controversy was so heated and why so many nationalistic overtones came into it.

It all started at Old Moshi when Gutmann was in Europe on leave and when Fritze of the neighbouring Mamba congregation was pastor in charge. He regularly attended the elders' meetings and distributed the sacraments; it was during a sacramental visit that Fritze triggered off the big controversy. A woman knelt down to receive Holy Communion, dressed well in European clothes and even wearing a hat.[66] Fritze took the hat off her head. High-handed actions of missionaries were not rare at that time and normally went unchallenged. But this time the woman involved was the wife of Joseph Merinyo who was perhaps the leading representative of the rising group of mostly mission educated Chagga who started to challenge the ruling position of the 'backward chiefs'. Through his position as clerk and translator for Charles Dundas and other British officials he had become influential in

---

[65] The *kanzu* is the men's dress, mostly of white material. It is of Arabic origin and was introduced into Kilimanjaro towards the end of the second half of the 19th century.
[66] Paul Fleisch, *Hundert Jahre lutherischer Mission*, p. 433.

Chagga politics. He was very progressive.[67] This was particularly evident in the fact that he was one of the founders of the cooperative movement on Kilimanjaro (KNPA) and its first secretary. Furthermore, as a boy he had been to Germany, he knew Swahili, English and German, and he was simply not willing to accept any innate difference between Europeans and Africans.

Merinyo's reaction was strong.[68] He wrote a long letter in German to the Leipzig Board complaining.[69] In this letter Merinyo first described how the Gospel came to Kilimanjaro and how many Chagga accepted it. He then described how other strangers also came (settlers, traders) who started to deprive the Chagga of what they had, and that after some time even some of the missionaries began to behave in the same way. They barred the Chagga from progress and together "with their uneducated church elders" they made laws about what clothes Christians had to wear. Then followed accusations of individual missionaries culminating in the complaint about Fritze:

"Therefore he begins with his own laws regarding dress and forces the people to follow his unpleasant laws, the worst he has done is this: The wife of Merinyo, the famous man of the Wachagga, he has taken off her hat and thrown it down without asking her or her husband."

The letter closes with the demand that Africans should be ordained as pastors, and a list of 13 teachers included who were said to have the confidence of the Christians and to be fit for ordination for the Christian ministry. For Moshi two were named: Yohane Kimambo and Petro Masamu, but not Imanuel Mkony.

The Leipzig Board did not send a written reply to Merinyo,[70] but reminded the missionaries that all matters of dress were an *adiaphoron* and should not be treated at all in a legalistic way.[71] Since Merinyo was such an influential man and Fritze's action was like the strong wind that fanned the flames of a long smouldering fire, the upheaval spread all over Eastern Chagga. In order to extinguish what he felt to be a dangerous fire, Superintendent Raum organized an official visitation to Mamba, Mwika and Old

---

[67] I.N. Kimambo and A.J. Temu (eds.), *A History of Tanzania*, Nairobi: EAPH, 1969, p. 137 (Iliffe) and Interview Merinyo 4.1970.
[68] For more detail see Anza Amen Lema, The Impact of the Leipzig Lutheran Mission on the People of Kilimanjaro, p. 442. He writes that Merinyo had complained first to Raum, Superintendent of the Mission, who wrote back advising Merinyo to discuss the matter with Fritze (Raum - Merinyo, May 1930). Merinyo claims that Fritze refused to talk to him, but a letter from Fritze in Merinyo's files dated 31.3.1930 inviting Merinyo "to discuss the matter" suggests that it may have been the other way round.
[69] Merinyo - Leipzig Board 8.5.1930.
[70] Interview Joseph Merinyo 4.1970.
[71] Leipzig Board - missionary council 12.8.1930.

Moshi and took Ittameier with him.[72] They were happy to ascertain that everywhere the "congregations as such had not been touched by Merinyo's agitation".[73] The ordinary Christians were still 'good Christians' and Raum chose the 1930 Church Conference at Mamba to deal publicly with Merinyo and so stop the 'agitation'. He was supposed to appear with his supporters, but he had to appear alone, as his supporters had meanwhile declared that they had already withdrawn their support. Raum was triumphant.[74]

Fritze also felt obliged to play an active role in quelling the rebellion. When the matter was discussed at the missionary conference, he understood that as missionary in charge of Old Moshi, he should take action against Merinyo. The opposite actually was decided and recorded in the minutes, namely that with this discussion the matter was finished and that Merinyo's complaint against Fritze should be discussed by the elders' meeting at Old Moshi in the presence of Fritze.[75] This meeting did not take place but soon Fritze received an anonymous letter accusing Merinyo of adultery. When Merinyo did not appear at a session of the elders,[76] he was excommunicated on the suspicion of adultery.[77] It was also stated that in case he should not be guilty of adultery the matter of his agitation would have to be taken up before readmitting him to communion.[78]

He protested against this excommunication in a blunt letter to Superintendent Raum. He received a friendly reply from Raum, but no action was taken.[79] Early in 1931 Merinyo's wife gave birth to a child and the parents wanted the child to be baptized. This was refused and the child was baptized by the Catholics.[80]

When Gutmann heard of the affair while still in Germany, he understood it much better than Raum and Fritze who were on the spot. He feared that a major African Independent Church might split off from Leipzig Mission as a

---

[72] Visitation report Mamba, Mwika, Old Moshi 18-24.7.1930 (Raum and Ittameier).
[73] Fritze sees this differently in annual report Mamba 1930.
[74] Raum - Leipzig Board 2.9.1930.
[75] Minutes elders 13.12.1932.
[76] Minutes elders 8.9.1930.
[77] J.B. Webster, *The African Churches among the Yoruba 1888-1922*, Oxford: Clarendon, 1964, p. 58, claims that the accusation of immorality was often used by missionaries against insubordinate or seceding Africans.
[78] Minutes elders 13.10.1930, 30.12.1930, 27.1.1931.
[79] Minutes elders 13.12.1932.
[80] Minutes elders 27.4.1931, 27.7.1931.

result of these troubles.[81] As possible reasons for this Gutmann saw the fact that several missionaries ruled their congregations too paternalistically.[82]

When he returned from Europe, one of his first tasks was to rectify the wrong that Fritze and Raum had done to Merinyo. He raised the matter again in the missionary council and was authorized to reinstate Merinyo into full church membership under the condition that he agreed that it was a mistake to let his child be baptized by the Catholics. To this Merinyo agreed and he was reinstated in December 1932.[83]

In this controversy we see Merinyo as the representative of the progressives defending their aspirations against a conservative missionary. But the important aspects is the difference between Fritze and Gutmann. Neither of them liked Africans to wear European dress.[84] But Gutmann was primarily concerned that the church should be properly related to the Chagga social order (e.g. the primal ties), whereas Fritze fought to preserve Chagga folklore. Gutmann demanded that all decisions in the congregations should be the result of a consultative process, whereas Fritze acted authoritatively. His insistence that the Chagga should not wear European dress was in fact not deference to Chagga culture but the result of European superiority. Gutmann was well aware that the *kanzu* was only a recent acquisition from the Arabs and he was convinced that the dress belonged to the outer fringe of a nation's culture. Therefore he preferred to come to terms with Merinyo's view instead of fighting losing battles over the adiaphoron of dress.[85]

In a similar way Gutmann accommodated himself to a far more important institution, the cooperative. His attitude becomes obvious in connection with the coffee riots of September 1937. These coffee riots were a reaction to a

---

[81] Ihmels - Gutmann 12.7.1930; cf. Bruno Gutmann, "Sektenbidung und Rasseerlebnis in Ostafrika", *Evangelisches Missionsmagazin*, 1934, pp. 227-292.

[82] Ihmels - Gutmann 12.7.1930. The situation was worst in Arusha where Leonhard Blumer had a controversy over dress and modernity with his congregation over a period of at least four years. As a punishment for the congregation's misbehaviour' Blumer again and again closed the church on Sunday and once his wife even nailed the door shut to prevent anyone from reopening it. When Blumer had severely beaten the pregnant wife or Lazaros Laiser, caretaker of the congregation, Leipzig recalled him to Germany on the suggestion of the missionary council in order to prevent the destruction of the congregation (Gutmann - missionary council 29.12.1933; Raum - Ihmels 1.1.1934; Superintendent Fuchs - Leipzig 4.12.1933). See also Max Pätzig, *Lasaros Laiser*, Erlangen, 1959, pp. 14-15.

[83] A more vivid description based on Interview Suzan Geiger Rogers - Stefano Moshi 7.7.1967 and Merinyo - Rogers 19.2.1970 is given in Suzan Geiger Rogers, The Search for Political Focus on Kilimanjaro, pp. 447-448.

[84] See Gutmann, *Freies Menschentum aus ewigen Bindungen*, p. 66 and Georg Fritze, "Die Kleiderfrage", *Evangelisches Missionsblatt*, 1928, pp. 248-252. See also on Gutmann: Ernst Johanssen, *Führung und Erfahrung im vierzigjährigen Missionsdienst*, II, p. 146. Also minutes elders 5.11.1929.

[85] For Gutmann's attitude to Merinyo's trip to Europe and to his excommunication in 1912 see *Evangelisches Missionsblatt*, 1913, p. 323.

sudden fall in coffee prices caused by the flooding of the market with Brazilian coffee. A number of coffee go downs were destroyed during these riots.[86] These outbursts occurred only in Protestant areas of Kilimanjaro,[87] but not at Old Moshi.[88] The centre of the agitation was Machame where Salomon Nkya, one of the two African pastors, strongly supported the agitation against the government backed unpopular rules of the KNCU and where the missionary took a neutral stand.[89] Though Gutmann used all his influence to put out the 'fire of agitation' against the cooperative movement at Old Moshi, this did not mean that he was a supporter of it.

In his many books and articles, Gutmann does not mention, even once, the cooperative movement. This is even more astonishing, as Merinyo, its first secretary, lived just half an hour downhill from Gutmann's house. Though Gutmann could not share Merinyo's view of society, he always remained on speaking terms with him. Why then did he not mention the cooperative movement? In one of his letters as Superintendent he revealed the reason: For him the cooperative movement was a dangerous thing. Not that he wanted to cement white domination, but as he saw the movement being rooted outside traditional Chagga society it was likely to cause disruption. He wrote:

> Such organizations here and everywhere become the arena for the aspirations and ambitions of those half-educated Africans who feel themselves to be more or less independent of traditional Chagga authority. And if in training and guiding them we do not succeed in making them immune against these dangers, the teachers, whether employed by government or missions, will always be the first victims and I have the impression that even in our own circles one has not realized the danger fully.[90]

Following this line of reasoning Gutmann tried to stem the tide. He fully supported the chief[91] and all traditional authority, and, because of his strong

---

[86] For a detailed analysis of the events: Suzan Geiger Rogers, The Search for Political Focus on Kilimanjaro, pp. 578-656 describes the events from 1935 to 1937, pp. 657-681 the coffee riots themselves. On the beginning of the movement see: pp. 263-292.
[87] Bruno Gutmann - Ihmels 1.10.1937.
[88] Ibid. 9.12.1936. Gutmann writes to Ihmels that when the agitation started to spread to Old Moshi, he had used all his influence to suppress it. Gutmann's account of the riots is: Letters Gutmann - Ihmels 22.9.1937 and 1.10.1937.
[89] Gutmann - Ihmels 9.12.1936 and annual report Salomon Nkya 1936.
[90] Gutmann (acting superintendent) - Ihmels 9.12.1936.
[91] That he did so with success is started in letter Küchler - Ihmels 16.10.1937.

influence, the cooperative movement gained little ground at Old Moshi.[92] That he had taken the right position was proven to him by that what happened at Machame (where Raum and the missionaries before him supported coffee growing very much)[93] did not happen at Old Moshi. True, destruction was avoided and people were spared from disturbances, but which way did Gutmann show for the future? Nothing but the support for waning traditional authorities. He proved that this was still viable, but he did not indicate for how long. This was a major problem for cultural conservatism everywhere in Tanzania. It was well related to traditional customs, social order and political authority, but in the ideology of cultural conservatism there was little provision of how to integrate social change and new aspirations.

6. Gutmann and the Progressives

The preceding sections demonstrate that Gutmann was not the arch tribalist he has often been depicted as being. Even towards institutions, which could possibly be dangerous to his conservative approach, like the schools, he did not develop a negative attitude. The same applies to the leading persons among the progressives. Though he did not share their aspirations he always maintained good relationships with them and retained their esteem. This is as much a witness to the strength of his personality as to the maturity, which his concepts had reached.

But still the basic difference between Gutmann and the progressive segment of Chagga society remained. Just as the colonial authorities identified with the traditional élite, so he also identified with them. Nevertheless there were important differences in degree. The most important was his conscious support for the training of pastors. With their ordination a new power structure emerged which was based on achieved role, as was the power structure of the missionaries and the colonial service. Prior to 1940 this structure only had limited powers, but it was ready to take over more responsibility when the German missionaries left. The same applies at the level of congregational leadership. True, he gave almost all authority to the elders. But at least two teachers and the full time staff of the congregation always belonged to its elders' council. In addition, the fact that Gutmann met every Friday with the teacher evangelists provided them with another avenue of influence. Though

---

[92] Visitation report Küchler 1937. It must be borne in mind that Gutmann was not supporting KNCU as against KNPA as was the case with government officials, he was equally critical of both as they had no roots in the traditional social order.
[93] Raum granted much more independence to the congregation (Küchler - Ihmels 16.10.1937).

Gutmann did not, on the whole, go far enough, he did achieve some integration of leadership concepts based on ascriptive and non-ascriptive roles.

Indirect Rule foresaw no development at all of the political institutions beyond the size of one 'tribe'. Even the church with its insistence on the vernacular was heavily focussed on the tribe, but still, right from the start an extra-tribal focus existed as the Lutheran Church that grew out of the work of the Leipzig Mission always comprised several ethnic groups. This 'super tribal' organization became tangible through the introduction of Church Conferences in 1930, and through the common training of candidates for ordination from all parts of the church in Swahili. In 1937 this focus was further extended by the creation of the Mission Church Federation, comprising Lutherans from all over Tanzania. All this means that at a time when the ideology of Indirect Rule focussed all energies on the 'tribes' the Lutheran Church already had a nationwide focus, dim though it may have been for the average church member at Old Moshi.

The end of the Era Gutmann

In 1938 Gutmann left for another leave in Germany. He was 62 years old and had become the Superintendent of the Mission. So it was decided to post him to Marangu, to coordinate the work of the Seminary and the whole educational system and to be the Superintendent of the Mission.[1] At Old Moshi Immanuel Mkony and Ndesanjo Kitange would continue their work as pastors, but it was still mission policy to put a German missionary in charge of the congregation, inexperienced as he may be.

Easter 1938 Gutmann introduced Ernst Jaeschke as his successor as pastor of Old Moshi congregation. At that time the congregation had 5500 members, comprising more than 25% of the population in its area. Jaeschke found all these many members of the congregation well organized, so that he felt, that though he was inexperienced, he could manage.[2] His service was cut short by the outbreak of the war, so that in 1940 he had to leave Old Moshi. Immanuel Mkony and Ndesanjo Kitange continued with the pastoral work.

Today Old Moshi-Mbokomu congregation does not exist as such any more. The church of Kidia is the bearer of much of the common history and the mother church, and is surrounded by her children: Mbokomu at over two hours distance, at a shorter distance Tela in the West and Sangu in the east, and not to forget her children in the mission field, Kahe and Uru in the plains. The Gospel has indeed taken root on Mt Kilimanjaro.

---

[1] It is incorrect to claim that due to his age and poor eye sight Gutmann decided in 1938 to remain in Germany to travel and speak for the Mission (Martin F. Shao, *Bruno Gutmann's Missionary Method and its Influence on the Evangelical Lutheran Church in Tanzania Northern Diocese*, Erlangen: Verlag der Ev.-Luth. Mission, 1990 (originally: MST, Wartburg Theological Seminary Dubuque, Iowa, 1985).

[2] Ernst Jaeschke, "Ein Leben für Afrikaner" in Bruno Gutmann, *Afrikaner-Europäer in nächstenschaftlicher Entsprechung. Gesammelte Aufsätze*, Stuttgart: Evangelisches Verlagswerk, 1966, p. 25.

Afterword

I was born and brought up in Germany, and after secondary school read theology at the Baptist Seminary in Hamburg, with the intention of becoming a missionary in South Tanzania, serving the Kanisa la Biblia there. Expecting to graduate from the Seminary at age 23, I felt a bit young and intended to study an extra year somewhere, maybe at Hamburg University. To my surprise Dr Luckey, the Principal of the Seminary, called me and advised me that I could take up the offer of an ecumenical scholarship for a year, somewhere abroad. I opted for any school in Tanzania, but on advice of the scholarship officer, then decided to study that year at Makerere University in Kampala, Uganda.

And that changed all my life. I did become a missionary in the Kanisa la Biblia, as I had intended, but there at Makerere, Prof Noel Q. King, then Head of Department of Religious Studies, discovered that I had academic abilities beyond the learning of the tools of my profession, and I discovered and experienced that fascination of research and scholarly work that has not left me ever since.

Fascinated as I was, I still had to get started with my academic work. Since my German qualification was difficult to assess according to East African standards, I was required to do one more academic year at Makerere to get my BA equivalent that would allow me to be registered for a higher degree. This was of course an MA, but I wanted to bypass that level and go for the PhD straight. In order to achieve the upgrading, after having done initial research, I drafted a history of Old Moshi-Mbokomu Evangelical Lutheran Church. I got my upgrading, and ultimately my PhD from the University of Dar es Salaam, but not for this essay, which I kept in my files. After many years, it came to the notice of a missionary pastor in that area, and he encouraged me to publish what was originally not intended for that purpose. When I asked him, if my history would be acceptable to the congregation, he replied, that there would be a good chance for that, though they might not agree with every detail.

Since by then I had written my thesis, which contained more material on the history of Old Moshi-Mbokomu,[3] I felt that I could supplement my origi-

---

[3] The thesis was: Klaus Fiedler, Conservative German Protestant Missionaries in Tanzania, 1900-1940. Written in English, it was first published in my German translation: Klaus Fiedler, *Christentum und afrikanische Kultur. Konservative deutsche Missionare in Tanzania, 1900-1940*, Gütersloh: Gütersloher Verlagshaus, 1983, ²1984, Bonn: VKW 1993, and only in 1996 in English, based on the original text:

nal essay from that source and thus produce a history covering all the time from the beginnings to 1940. I offer this little book to the congregation with my thanks for their hospitality, with many thanks that they preserved the historical records, and with my wishes that it may allow them to see some of what God did in their history.

Klaus Fiedler
Zomba, March 2006

Klaus Fiedler, *Christianity and African Culture. Conservative German Protestant Missionaries in Tanzania, 1900-1940*, Leiden: Brill, 1996.

Bibliography

Ayandele, E.A., The Missionary Impact on Modern Nigeria 1842-1994, London, 1966.

Beyerhaus, Peter, Die Selbständigkeit der jungen Kirchen, Wuppertal, 1956.

Burke, Edmund, Reflections on the Revolution in France, Harmondsworth: Penguin, 1969 (1790).

Cameron, Donald, "Native Administration in Nigeria and Tanganyika", Extra Supplement of the Journal of the Royal African Society, vol. 26, 1937.

Eggert, Johanna, Missionsschule und sozialer Wandel in Ostafrika, Bielefeld: Bertelsmann, 1970.

Fiedler, Klaus, "Bishop Lucas' Christianization of Traditional Rites, the Kikuyu Female Circumcision Controversy and the 'Cultural Approach' of Conservative German Missionaries in Tanzania", in Noel Q. King and Klaus Fiedler (eds.), Robin Lamburn – From a Missionary's Notebook: the Yao of Tunduru and other Essays, Saarbrücken/Ft. Lauderdale, 1991, pp. 207-217.

Fiedler, Klaus, Christianity and African Culture. Conservative German Protestant Missionaries in Tanzania, 1900-1940, Leiden: Brill, 1996; Blantyre: CLAIM-Kachere, 1999.

Fiedler, Klaus, The Story of Faith Missions. From Hudson Taylor to Present Day Africa, Oxford et al: 1994, ²1995.

Fleisch, Paul, Hundert Jahre lutherischer Mission, Leipzig: Verlag der Ev-Luth. Mission, 1936.

Fritze, Georg, "Die Kleiderfrage", Evangelisches Missionsblatt, 1928, pp. 248-252.

Gutmann, Bruno (ed), Kitabu kya siri [Book of the Congregation], Moshi/Mbokomu 1931.

Gutmann, Bruno (trsl.), Mkundana Mhya fu Mbike ni Mndumi odu Yesu Kristo, Stuttgart: Bibelanstalt 1939.

Gutmann, Bruno, "Brautexamen am Kilimandscharo" in Bruno Gutmann, Afrikaner - Europäer in nächstenschaftlicher Entsprechung. Gesammelte Aufsätze (ed. by Ernst Jaeschke), Stuttgart: Evangelisches Verlagswerk, 1966, pp. 192-196, originally published as: Gutmann, Bruno, "Brautexamen am Kilimandscharo", in Deutscher evangelischer Missions-Kalender 10, 1935, pp. 28-30.

Gutmann, Bruno, "Der Kampf um die Schulzucht", Evangelisches Missionsblatt, 1927, pp. 31-36.

Gutmann, Bruno, "Die gegenwärtige Lage der Dschaggamission", Jahrbuch der sächsischen Missionskonferenz, 1912, pp. 49-67.

Gutmann, Bruno, "Die Gemeinde", Das Gottesjahr, 1939, p. 56.

Gutmann, Bruno, "Eine Jugendlehre bei den Wadschagga", *Evangelisches Missionsblatt*, 1911, pp. 14-21.

Gutmann, Bruno, "Einweisung in den Hirtendienst an einer christlichen Gemeinde", published only in German translation, first in *Dorfkirche*, 1941, pp. 58ff, then, after the war, in *Lutherische Blätter*, 1960, no. 65, pp. 40-53. Most easily accessible in Gutmann, *Afrikaner - Europäer*, pp. 150-167.

Gutmann, Bruno, "Johane Kimambo, ein Jünger ohne Falsch", *Afrikanische Charakterköpfe: Unseres Heilands schwarze Handlanger*, Leipzig 1922.

Gutmann, Bruno, "Sektenbidung und Rasseerlebnis in Ostafrika", *Evangelisches Missionsmagazin*, 1934, pp. 227-292.

Gutmann, Bruno, "The African Standpoint", *Journal of the International Institute of African Languages and Cultures*, vol. 8, January 1935, no. 1, pp. 1-17.

Gutmann, Bruno, "Von Ihnen nach Außen – der lutherische Weg", *Evangelisch-Lutherische Kirchenzeitung*, 1954, pp. 305-309.

Gutmann, Bruno, "Wie ich den Buren begegnete", *Evg.-Luth. Missionsblatt*, 1905, pp. 330-334.

Gutmann, Bruno, *Afrikaner - Europäer in nächstenschaftlicher Entsprechung. Gesammelte Aufsätze (ed. by Ernst Jäschke)*, Stuttgart: Evangelisches Verlagswerk, 1966.

Gutmann, Bruno, *Anton Tarimo, der Evangelist von Moshi*, Leipzig: Verlag der Evg.-Luth. Mission, 1924, p. 16.

Gutmann, Bruno, *Christusleib und Nächstenschaft*, Feuchtwangen, 1931, pp. 37f.

Gutmann, Bruno, *Das Dschaggaland und seine Christen*, Leipzig: Verlag der Ev-Luth. Mission, 1925.

Gutmann, Bruno, *Die Stammeslehren der Dschagga*, 3 vols., München: C.H. Beck'sche Verlangsbuchhandlung, 1932, 1935, 1938.

Gutmann, Bruno, *Freies Menschentum aus ewigen Bindungen*, Kassel, 1928.

Gutmann, Bruno, *Gemeindeaufbau aus dem Evangelium*, Leipzig, 1925; .

Gutmann, Bruno, *Häuptling Rindi von Moshi - Ein Afrikanisches Helden- und Herrscherleben*, Köln, nd. (1928).

Gutmann, Bruno, *Unter dem Trutzbaum – Eine Einkehr in Moshi am Kilimanjaro*, Leipzig: Verlag der Ev.-Luth. Mission, nd. [1938], p. 71.

Gutmann, Bruno, *Zurück auf die Gottesstraße*, Leipzig, nd. (1938), p. 62.

Jaeschke, Ernst, "Ein Leben für Afrikaner" in Gutmann, Bruno, *Afrikaner-Europäer in nächstenschaftlicher Entsprechung. Gesammelte Aufsätze*, Stuttgart: Evangelisches Verlagswerk, 1966, pp. 11-31.

Jaeschke, Ernst, "Bruno Gutmann's Legacy", *Occasional Bulletin of Missionary Research*, October 1980.

Jaeschke, Ernst, *Gemeindeaufbau in Afrika. Die Bedeutung Bruno Gutmanns für das afrikanische Christentum*, Stuttgart: Calwer Verlag, 1981.

Johanssen, Ernst, "Heraus aus der Isolierung", *Neue Allgemeine Missionszeitschrift*, 1930.

Johanssen, Ernst, *Führung und Erfahrung im vierzigjährigen Missionsdienst*, 3 vols., Bethel: nd.

Kimambo, I.N. and A.J. Temu (eds.), *A History of Tanzania*, Nairobi: EAPH, 1969.

Lema, Anza Amen, The Impact of the Leipzig Lutheran Mission on the People of Kilimanjaro, PhD, University of Dar es Salaam, 1973.

Murray, Jocelyn, The Kikuyu Female Circumcision Controversy: with Special Reference to the Church Missionary Society's Sphere of Influence, PhD, UCLA, 1974.

Nicolson, Harold, *Peacemaking 1919*, revised edition 1943, reprinted 1967 (London).

Njau, Filipo, *Aus meinem Leben* (ed. Martin Küchler), Erlangen: Verlag der Evg.-Luth. Mission, 1960.

Oliver, Roland, *The Missionary Factor in East Africa*, 1967 (London, 1952). Edition.

Pätzig, Max, *Lasaros Laiser*, Erlangen, 1959.

Raum, Johannes, "Die Hirtenschule in Madschame", *Lutherisches Missionsjahrbuch*, 1934, pp. 142-149.

Raum, Johannes, "Heranbildung eingeborener Pastoren fur die Gemeinden der Evg.-Luth. Mission zu Leipzig in Ostafrika", *Neue Allgemeine Missionszeitschrift*, 1933, pp. 22-34.

Raum, Otto, *Chagga Childhood*, London: OUP, 1940.

Robinson, Kenneth, *The Dilemmas of Trusteeship*, London: OUP, 1965.

Shao, Martin F., *Bruno Gutmann's Missionary Method and its Influence on the Evangelical Lutheran Church in Tanzania Northern Diocese*, Erlangen: Verlag der Ev-Luth. Mission, 1990 (originally: MST, Wartburg Theological Seminary Dubuque, Iowa, 1985).

Stahl, Kathleen M., *History of the Chagga People of Kilimanjaro*, London 1964.

Sundkler, Bengt and Christopher Steed, *A History of the Church in Africa*, Cambridge University Press, ²2001.

Warneck, Gustav, *Abriß einer Geschichte der protestantischen Missionen von der Reformation bis auf die Gegenwart*, Berlin: Martin Warneck, 1910.

Warneck, Gustav, *Evangelische Missionslehre*, 5 vols., Gotha, 1897-1903.

Webster, J.B., *The African Churches among the Yoruba 1888-1922*, Oxford: Clarendon, 1964.

Winter, J.C., *Bruno Gutmann 1876-1966: a German Approach to Social Anthropology*, Oxford: 1979.

Wright, Marcia, German Evangelical Missions in Tanganyika, 1891-1939, with Special Reference to the Southern Highlands, PhD, London University, 1966, p. 347.

Wright, Marcia, German Missions in Tanganyika 1891-1941: Lutherans and Moravians in the Southern Highlands, Oxford: Clarendon, 1971, p. 178.

www.ingramcontent.com/pod-product-compliance
Lightning Source LLC
Chambersburg PA
CBHW021146230426
43667CB00005B/277